"Heaven or Hell" by Natalia Giordana

"With much love, this novel is dedicated to all who wish to be
saved".

Introduction
**"Consider your origins: you were not made to live as brutes,
but to follow virtue and knowledge".**
Dante Alighieri

Allegria was a woman under 30. She had a simple degree of beauty but not the sensual or typical attraction a beautiful woman can generate. Her main interest was to be intelligent and wise. That was the reason that made her unique. Allegria lived up to her name. She was a cheerful, joyful and always smiling woman; with a lot of inner life.

She was straightforward, sincere and direct, but at the same time pleasant, diligent and trusting. She was dynamic and loved to do things. She had an exciting life. She was the kind of woman who simultaneously knew how to be warm and cold. She knew when to be friendly and walk away if it was necessary. That's how Allegria's personality can be portrayed.

Allegria had set out to cross the border. She had to process some papers as she would travel to Denmark to live near her fiancé. It seemed like a typical day, a daily grind. Nothing different was going on. It was like those ordinary days when she got up, dressed, and set off to see nothing new, but the heavenly world had other plans for her.

She was crossing the border to do the paperwork and arrived at the place where she contacted some people who started to help her speed up the process until she found a fair-minded person to finish the process.

Allegria always smiles, trying to look nice while hearing the explanations of costs and the timeline for her papers. She began to speak to the proper officer in charge, Ariel Muller, the chief officer of the area who would complete the process. As Mr Muller was talking to her, her body began to weaken. She started to feel unwell; things changed suddenly, she began to feel sick, breaking out in a cold sweat, and her body shivered. She was unable to stand up properly and tried to hide her condition. She heard everything she needed to hear, said goodbye and went to the bathroom.

Once in the bathroom, she tries to keep her composure, but it worsens. She looks for water to refresh her face but can't find the faucet. She was beginning to lose track of reality. She sweats, sweats, sweats... she doesn't feel hot or cold. She starts to feel nothing but manages to get out of the bathroom and then collapses. The pulse is at zero. She seems dead, the heart stops beating, and Allegria starts to fly. All she sees is light, and she knows God is there. Her soul breaks away from her body, and it is in heaven.

An indescribable peace surrounds her. She's never felt so complete. Everything in heaven was peace and love. Everything was perfection, light, order, acceptance, and peace. There was love. Allegria was completely loved, as no human love can ever love. She was loved by heaven, by God himself.

In every corner of that experience, she sees only joy. There is no darkness. Everything is light. Allegria can see her body from heaven and speaks to God, saying, "I am dying, receive my soul, I am dying, the demons are killing me, the demons are destroying me, this is it, this is the end, it was not supposed to end like this, destroyed".

God, eternal peace, all light and whose pure essence is love, replies to her, "You are not going to die; not yet, you must return". Allegria sighs and argues, "It is so difficult. It is a war that even seems impossible. It is a war. The evil seems so strong". God caresses her face and, with love, tells her, "You must return, Allegria, my beloved; you must return and tell your story".

At that time, nothing mattered, neither human love, nor money, nor fame, not having everything, nor having nothing, to be or not to be... because absolutely everything was taken over by God; all that mattered was just God.

It was a sublime moment when life suddenly stopped, and it was when she contemplated what matters. The fact that she is breathing, able to absorb the infinite and the feeling of not being willing to go back. It was a time when Allegria's humanity was caressing the creator of the universe, who is beyond all the barriers of time and space. It was a time when she understood the omnipotence and sublimity of the one who is all, and God made her feel so fragile and marvellous at the same time. This perfect God is everything and does not reject anyone but spreads His love.

Allegria, with deep love and devotion, kneels and exclaims, "I love you, God!".

When she started to die, it was the exact moment she was in heaven and spoke to God. Allegria had been through a fainting spell and did not react to the paramedic's first aid treatment.

However, Allegria had to come back because her time had not passed. She had to do something before leaving for eternity, and that's what God told her to do; God told her to share her story.

At that moment, Allegria's body began to receive medical attention because she had suffered a heart attack.

The medical corps began the recapture process, and Allegria started to react. Little by little, everything comes back to life. The pulse returns and the heart starts to beat again. They decided to admit her, so she was transferred to "Umberto Parini" Hospital, the public hospital in Aosta, where she would be observed.

While in the ambulance, Allegria only thought about her experience and what she had lived. All the time she spent in the hospital, she only thought about how sublime God was and that she should obey him, so she decided to tell her story, knowing that her whole story might help someone else.

When Giovanni visited Allegria, she said, "My love, I will begin to write. I will tell my story". Giovanni smiled and kissed her. Giovanni was a man full of love and replied, "Awesome, go ahead, darling, do it!". Whenever Allegria saw Giovanni, she thought, "God is merciful" because Giovanni was such a good man, so calm, that he only knew how to bring happiness and goodness to Allegria's heart. Giovanni was a gift from God for the life of Allegria. He knew how to give peace and calm to her life.

"In the beginning, God created the heavens and the earth. Now the earth was formless and empty, darkness was over the surface of the deep, and the Spirit of God was hovering over the waters. And God said, "Let there be light," and there was light. God saw that the light was good, and he separated the light from the darkness" (Genesis 1:1-4).

We will initiate this story with "Let there be light". Let there be light in our minds, intellects, feelings, and hearts... let there be light in our lives because the light separates the darkness.

Laws govern the universe; some of us may know them, and some may ignore them, but this does not remove the fact that we will all receive the weight of the law.

Ignorance of the law does not deprive us of its consequences, and just as there are universal, material, scientific and human laws, there are spiritual laws. For a person to ignore spiritual laws will not deprive him of their consequences.

We will all be judged based on the spiritual laws that God has decreed, and a person who denies the existence of God does not deprive God of His presence or of being the absolute ruler of the universe. Someone ignoring God doesn't take God off the scene.

Whether you like it or not, everyone must answer to God, indicating whether we spend eternity in heaven... or hell.

The law (in Latin, lex, legis) is a legal norm dictated by the legislator, a precept established by the competent authority, in which something is ordered or prohibited by justice, the non-compliance with it leads to a sanction. It can be said that law is the external control of human behaviour.

"Ignorantia juris non exist" or "ignorant legis neminem exist," from the Latin "ignorance does not exempt from compliance with the law". It is a principle of law that indicates that ignorance or unawareness of the law does not serve as an excuse because it governs the necessary legal presumption that, having been enacted, everyone should know it.

European law countries with a Roman law tradition may also use an expression by Aristotle translated into Latin: "Nemo censer ignorare legem", that is, "nobody is thought to be ignorant of the law" or "ignorantia iuris nocet"; that means, "not knowing the law is harmful".

As for the ignorance of subjective and proper law, the Romans admitted some cases that produced concrete effects. Authors usually distinguish ignorance from the error of law by saying that the former is a total ignorance of the law and the latter a false and incomplete knowledge, but the distinction is irrelevant in practice.

Before God, the Judge of judges, we shall all be judged.

"Causa judicative individua est" translates as "the thing judged is indivisible." We must all come individually before God and cannot give excuses; we will be judged separately and held accountable for our body, soul and spirit.

We all have a conscience that accuses us and dictates what is wrong and what we should do so that no one can give suitable excuses before God.
This was something that Allegria, Costantino, and Giovanni had to be aware of.
Because on this earth, everyone deals with choice. You will need to choose where you will go to spend eternity, whether in heaven... or hell.

Chapter 1
"First step to hell"
"All hope abandon, ye who enter here!".
Dante Alighieri

It was the 1990s, ten years earlier, when Allegria had passed out. The '90s was the decade of pop and where we all connected, where the triumph of liberal democracies over communism was established. Yes, that decade! Allegria was 20 years old and listened to music on her Walkman while chewing gum and blowing bubbles. She was dreamy but normal. She believed in an extraordinary future but didn't know what awaited her.

She longed for a great future, unaware she was about to enter a great hell. It was as if hell had been waiting to hunt her down. It was as if all the hidden dangers had been waiting for her in the shadows, ready to attack her.

A deadly attack was coming for the lovely Allegria.

She got an invitation from a pop group. It wasn't "the super mega pop group". Those standard pop groups were neither fun nor fabulous as far as the musical revolution of the time was concerned, but they certainly had a long list of followers.

They were like bands formed with college friends who initially were amateurs but became pros. It wasn't the band; it was the style. It wasn't because they were so transcendent in their songs but because of what they meant. The band would make children, young people, adults and even the elderly jump and chant. It was those bands that you don't know why, but they have everything, not everything you could desire, but everything people want.

Not convinced but attracted by the idea of being able to "jump, dance and enjoy in a group", Allegria decided to go to that concert. Allegria wears her black nylon stockings, her denim skirt, a pink T-shirt on her body and she tied her hair with a pompom, yes, something horrible for our decade but let's understand that it was the nineties and at that time she was wearing it like almost all the girls.

She goes with friends; Laura, Nicola and Marcella.

Laura was sensational, with a beautiful smile that captivated everyone. She wore a novel flowery dress, not bad at all.

Nicola was sweet and warm, tender inside and in all her forms. That day she surprised her friends by wearing waist jeans (she never wore jeans).

Marcella was sexy by nature, her way of laughing, her body and curves, her way of walking, her way of posing. She would always look radiant in any outfit; at any age. She was an everlasting princess!

They went to the concert, and you could imagine hearing the playbacks from; "What is love? Baby don't hurt me, don't hurt me, no more" (Haddaway); "The summer is magic, is magic oh, oh, oh" (Playahitti), to; "I like to move it, move it" (Real 2 Real).

Although that would be entering the pop scene in a secular concert, the concert that Allegria was going was in a church, so it would only sound like Christian pop since Allegria was a fan of the church and her whole world was about Jesus.

Everything was expected. It was a concert like any other, in the dark, with lights on the stage, shouting, jumping and dancing. The preview was lived out full of enthusiasm. Singular bands were playing and preparing the audience until an extraordinary moment came.

It was boiling, and Allegria's friends advised her to go upstairs to the stands so they wouldn't be so tight in the crowd. So, Laura, Nicola and Marcella led Allegria to the right place. It should be noted that it became the right place for the big moment, not when the band appeared, but for the big moment that would mark Allegria's life.

A moment she would think would be her introduction to heaven, but in reality, it was like the snare of the Fowler. It was the first moment she would put her feet down, taking her first step towards her long journey to hell.

Everything was dark, and the moment came when the band would appear. Silence, breathing, anxiety and explosion! The band started with their major hit, and everyone started screaming because of the madness of being able to hear them. The band seems, and the auditorium explodes. Stage lights and the big moment arrives; Costantino sees Allegria, and Allegria discovers Costantino.

Heaven explodes, and hell, Costantino and Allegria meet. It was those events where everything was dark, and suddenly, there were three seconds of light, but those three seconds were enough to meet the love of your life. At that moment, the gates of hell began to open for Allegria, and she innocently began to take her first step into the darkness.

When he saw Allegria, Costantino observed the most beautiful of the creatures in the human race. He was not only attracted by the physical but also by all her essence. He was captivated by everything that Allegria transmitted, by everything she was. The idea is monstrous but true; hell is attracted to capture heaven and is always pleased to sully the holy and pure ones.

This was the case. In the parallel world, it was heaven versus hell, but in the real world, both looked and seemed part of heaven, as if destined to live a heavenly story.

Allegria, at the sight of Costantino, believes that heaven opened up and a beautiful, precious angel who seems to be everything and bestowed with everything. It was like Allegria's eyes were opened, and now she could see another world hadn't seen before!

It was like a different sensory experience like she was moving to another world, and three seconds were enough to look at herself, not see herself, but look into his eyes and soul.

As Katy Perry would say, "You're so hypnotising; could you be evil? Could you be an angel?.... feels like I am floating, leaves my body glowing... you're not like the others, futuristic lover, different DNA, they don't understand you".

Exactly as Allegria was experiencing it, "You're from a whole other world, a different dimension, you open my eyes, and I'm ready to go, lead me into the light", and in those three seconds, she was ready to be infected with the love of this angel and feel all her poison.

Everything she was feeling was supernatural, extraterrestrial, out of this world, extrasensory. Let's face it; unnatural experiences can come from God or the devil.

Allegria felt as if she had visited or been in another world, in a dimension she did not know, but she did not know if that was good or bad because he could be an angel... or a devil.

A Godsent being or a fallen angel. At that point, she didn't know he was a fallen angel. She decided not to think so much about whether it was good or bad, as she overestimated how she felt. Everything seems to be transcendental, not just any experience, but "the experience".

Haven't they ever told you that feelings could be deceiving? Well, that's what was happening. She was falling into hell. It will take time for her to discover that that experience will be a deception.

As Katy Perry would say: "This is transcendental, on another level, boy, you're my lucky star". So Allegria felt like she had been experiencing the light of his star on another level.

Although Allegria would have to be told that before experimenting with that star, she should ensure she knew if that light and that experience came from God. However, it was a "church" concert with a "church" band; what could be wrong? What could be harmful if it was all within the place where you find just goodness? In that supernatural experience, Allegria didn't notice that there was a shadow next to so much light, and that shadow was sitting next to Costantino.

Allegria felt she had been introduced into the light; however, what kind of light? Did you never think of the phrase "not all that glitters is gold"? However, how could you believe it wasn't gold if everything looked so bright in front of your eyes?

She had seen a vision; it was supernatural, and everything was full of light; what could have gone wrong?

This whole experience was in three seconds. It's amazing what love can do to you, right? Another planet, another dimension, supernatural experiences. Are humans so sensitive or fragile that we all become enlightened before love?

The three seconds were up, and they had to get back to reality, and reality was shouting, "Allegria, Allegria! Do you want some popcorn?". Laura said she was hungry, and the popcorn seller was passing by. Allegria thought the last thing she would care about was eating, so she smiled and said, "No, thank you!"

In the continuous bleachers upwards, Costantino sat behind Allegria, offering to buy something for his new friends. The seller looked out and offered "Sweets, gum, chocolates, popcorn", and another surprise appeared. Laura, Nicola and Marcella seem to know him.

As the old saying goes, the twists and turns of life, "Birds of the feather flock together". That is true; people who have similar characteristics or interests come together. Costantino seemed to be one more of the many, one more among the friends... and maybe that's the problem. He was the well-known Costantino who worked in a crowded bookstore, so they greeted him as if they had known each other long ago.

Allegria could barely utter three words in a row while trying to understand what had happened. Many emotions experienced in three seconds were not ubiquitous in her deep world.

Costantino buys what his friends suggest: cookies, chips, gum, and candies. We know how women's cravings can be. Costantino seemed like the perfect gentleman any woman would have expected, so perfect that it didn't seem authentic. Maybe he wasn't true. Perhaps he wasn't even real.

Everyone continues to enjoy the concert, the great show. Suddenly, the first conversation arises as Costantino stands right the next row after Allegria. He goes over to her right shoulder and whispers, "Hello, I'm Costantino," she turns and smiles, saying: "Nice to meet you. I'm Allegria" "Allegria, what a beautiful name, a name that I hope will fully meet the reality of the adjective" "Yes, my name it's a name with history, inspired by Mary, the mother of Jesus, a woman who brought much joy to Christianity". Costantino smiles as he looks at her complacently.

Allegria, unable to bear the silence between them, says, "I see, my friends know you. Do you work in a bookstore?" "Yes, that's what I do, in general", he replies, "I imagine you like reading", says Allegria, "Of course, I do. I read a lot. One of my favourite writers is Max Lucado". Allegria smiles, brightening her face, and says, "Oh, he's one of my favourites, too! Wow, what a coincidence!" replies Costantino.

Surprised by the answer, Costantino says, "Wow! We have that in common". Allegria nods and meditates on the works of this writer, remembering that her favourite book was "Applause from Heaven".

Allegria, intrigued if the coincidence went further, asks Costantino which of this author's books was his favourite and, to her surprise, he answers, "Applause from heaven". As if he had read her mind, he even said that the book encouraged him a lot in his life as if it seemed that the angel of Costantino was destined... to heaven.

Although time would show that Costantino was an angel with more desires from hell than heaven. Of course, the naive woman of Allegria did not know that. She could not see the shadow that was settled in Costantino. She could not discern it or see the shadow he carried behind him. She could not see or understand anything because she was head over heels in love.

Poor Allegria was so young and eager to fall in love that it seemed fate had crossed them, but what fate would it be, God's or the devil's?

God wants it to be on "earth as it is in heaven"; however, the devil likes it to be on "earth as it is in hell". Costantino seemed good, full of light that you would never imagine his life would be a perfect example of "on earth as it is in hell".

Allegria didn't want to think about shadows. She was in heaven. The sky had opened up. She had seen a vision, and an angel had come to her world. How could we think of hell at such a good time when it was only experiencing light and joy; we could even say, love!

God is love. It is supposed that when you are experiencing love, you are experiencing God Himself, and everything that comes from love is good, pleasant and perfect. At least she was thinking like that. She forgot the rest of the Bible at that point. Unfortunately, of course, Allegria did not imagine that love is pure and that sometimes love can begin as something pure and then degrade, degenerate and corrupt itself. Sometimes, what starts as something good gradually becomes something bad, excruciating.

Nevertheless, let's put these ideas aside and see how the night went. Before the end of the concert, the friends rushed out to avoid being stuck in the parking lot. They pushed Allegria to say goodbye during their pleasant conversation and diplomatically forced her out.

Allegria nodded and said, "Well, it was a pleasure, Costantino" "The pleasure, it's all mine". They look into each other's eyes, smiling, blushing and somewhat embarrassed. They seem so pure at the time.

That typical shyness when love comes to the door for the first time. You could even feel that sexual tension or that fatal attraction of first love when you don't know whether to kiss his cheek, give him a tender hug, hold his hand, or kiss him on those red lips.

Allegria was very timid at that moment. She says goodbye with a quick "ciao" without giving a chance to anything else and runs away from the place after her friends.

When the friends left the venue, they made fun of Allegria. Laura said, "Wow, we all saw you chatting very comfortably. You even seemed to like each other". Allegria smiles shyly and says, "C'mon, girls, we were just chatting!".

That 'we just chatted' in Allegria's mind meant 'we like each other from the first moment. Love at first sight, because as it is already known, when a woman says one thing, she means something else, the opposite". Women never say what they think. Women always say what they feel; men always say what they think and never say what they feel. God made us different but complementary, which is the secret of being one.

After the concert, Costantino was thinking about what he had experienced, too. He thought he had seen the sun or the moon; he was captivated by the beauty of Allegria, but such beauty was not desirable. Of course, it was desirable, absolutely alluring. Still, if Allegria was desirable, Costantino could not say that to the shadow because next to Costantino, there was the shadow, and the shadow did not let him think or meditate about pure love.

The shadow wanted to grow in Costantino's heart; moreover, it was growing, so the shadow wanted to overwhelm goodness and silence any feeling of tenderness or sweet reaction that he might have towards Allegria.

Costantino arrived home and thought about how desirable Allegria was. The friendly and spontaneous Allegria, but he wouldn't dare to tell it to the shadow because the shadow would get mad.

The shadow wanted to grow, tried to take over goodness, wanted to attack, and the shadow thought it would attack if Costantino had the idea of loving, longing or wishing Allegria.

The shadow would come for his soul... and finish him and Allegria. The shadow had no mercy. Hatred is his weapon; his plan was always to kill, steal, destroy and make this unique plan in Costantino's life: "I want everything, and I would come for everything; I want his soul, and if in the process I have to finish with Allegria, I wouldn't hesitate to do so".

***

Allegria was tossing and turning in bed, repeatedly reviewing everything that had happened that night. Allegria could not sleep from the excitement when she arrived home; she had seen the most handsome man on earth, and he was real! Costantino, his kindness, appearance, warmth, and entire personality. For that moment, everything before the eyes of Allegria shone and looked like gold.

Costantino's sky-blue eyes reflected such peace that Allegria could not imagine that they would disguise any shadow, the most terrible shadow.

For his part, Costantino thought the same thing. In the dark eyes of Allegria, he felt her eyes looked like shadows, but they were not like an evil shadow; on the contrary, they were bright and expressive, full of life as if they mirrored only joy when you looked at them.

Costantino was captivated by this lady even though he knew that the shadow would not allow him to be happy with her, but he still wanted to dream of a night when he could be pleased with her. Happiness? A word that was not frequent in Costantino's life. Satisfaction is what he longed to find with Allegria.

Although the shadow had once promised him that he would be happy someday, and now that the years have passed, it seems that Costantino has never been pleased, neither before, nor with Allegria, nor with the shadow.

How can he be delighted if he has given his life to the shadow? And the shadow can never deliver what it doesn't have; the shadow has no joy, no peace, no true love, nothing at all; the shadow is just that, a shadow of what it represents: hell.

However, it was too early for us to spoil the party. Let them dream that they can be happy, that their plans can be shaped and work.

It is said that what stops dreams are the realities, the harsh reality, and maybe that is the shadow, the infernal reality, but imagine that dreams may come true.

The next day, Allegria wakes up and calls her friend Laura to discuss everything that happened the night before. Of course, the phones weren't like ours. They were those of the '90s, one spoke using a tube attached to a circular cable, a telephone line, and to dial-up, one had to turn a numbered disc; yes, welcome to the '90s! Laura was waiting for Allegria's call, not because she loved gossiping but because that's how women are; they need to talk about everything! Laura got the ring, and she first said, "Allegria, yesterday you met your destiny!" but Allegria replied, "Mmm, I don't know if that's the case. Well, how do I know?", "Oh, I think you're just right for each other. You're both tender, sensitive, art-loving and friendly. We gotta arrange to visit him at the bookstore!".

However, Allegria, quite balanced head, replied, "Lau, aren't you just overexcited about this?" Laura pushed on and continued, "Well, darling, you would never know until you try it, so let's just go for it! Allegria, I saw how he looked at you. You attracted him so badly, and you're nerdy as far as men are concerned; trust me, my boyfriend looked at me just like he did, and now we're about to get married! So, girl, don't play dumb or slow. That's how it starts. You have to attack. It's your turn. You greet, you talk and wait for his reactions".

Allegria, quite naive, took some time to digest everything she had just heard and replied, "Wow, it seems that I am talking to the expert of the friends' club, the mentor for action", Laura mocking Allegria, replied, "Of course, girl, because if the rest of us would go at your speed, we might get married at the second coming of Christ. Girl, the real world is faster now. Girl, if you don't follow my advice, you will remain out there to dress saints, and you have to be aware that there are few saints left out there if there are any. So, darling, I don't know if you may find someone to dress".

Allegria was naive but with a good sense of humour, just smiling, thinking that maybe her friend was right.

It is clear that Laura had a great sense of humour, so with her very personal and unique style, she convinced Allegria to go to the bookstore and find out how the story goes.

Costantino was doing the same thing, discovering who this "Allegria Disalvatore" was.

In the '90s, you could not google the name of a person, no Facebook, no WhatsApp or social networks.

In the '90s, you had to ask a friend who was a friend of a friend who was close to the family to find out about someone that you fancied. Yes, it was a matter of word of mouth, and that's how you learned more about someone.

Following the methods of the 90s, Costantino called a friend who knew he had a friend who knew a friend who was a friend of a friend of the Disalvatore family.

A mafia-like system where you get to know everything because everything follows a chain, a sequence of contacts, but it wasn't a mafia; it was just the 90s!

The Disalvatore family was a typical Italian family: united, affectionate, and joyful. Alberto Disalvatore was an exemplary father, philosopher, theologian and creative. The same could be said of her mother, Giulia, an example of a virtuous woman.

Alberto Disalvatore was a teacher and pastor, and he was passionate about God and football. When his dear Juventus was playing, the activities in the house stopped. Alberto loved being with people, serving them, talking about God, and helping others; he lived for the church where he worked. He liked good wine and good meat, eating delicious pizzas and the classic gnocchi, ravioli and lasagna every Sunday. The whole family enjoyed the "buon piacere".

Giulia was an excellent cook, a house-lover, and the kind of mother everyone would like to have. Allegria had a brother and sister. Brother Giuseppe was an entrepreneur by nature. He was always creating something, repairing something. He was an engineer full of competence and cunning. He was also good at skiing and playing football.

Allegria's sister Beatrice was a superstar known for her beauty and kindness. She loved to enjoy her life, and just as Dante Alighieri loved Beatrice so much, Beatrice was very much loved by her husband, Carlo.

The Disalvatore family lived up to their surname. They belonged to the Savior, and everything in that house was light and peaceful. The big family always shared the holy Sundays.

Allegria lived in a beautiful and historic house on the Via Roma in Valle d'Aosta, Italy. Remember that almost everything in Italy has a historical past, as it is the cradle of a culture as significant as the one in the Roman Empire. Allegria's home had beautiful antique decorations.

Allegria's grandparents were born there, in the cradle of skiing and mountaineering. The Piedmontese culture is rich in its rights regarding cuisine, drinking habits and dressing style.

Allegria used to visit Turin and Milan, which were very close to their place. Milan is the centre of international fashion, so the whole of Italy is always up-to-date when it comes to style.

Allegria loved the history of the Roman Empire because everything around her reminded her of where she had come from. She had a great love for Italy and all its culture. In her spare time, she loves reading about Rome and, the Second World War, Mussolini, because it was a topic of question for her.

Allegria was living in Aosta. The Alps surround the city. In winter, the snow whitens the whole place. The people are warm and cheerful, and everyone cares for each other. It's like a small town, and almost everyone knows each other.

Waking up in the morning with the impressive sun and seeing the Alps was an absolute visual delight for Allegria. The churches are ancient, and the bells of each church toll every hour to the musical sound, reminding people of the time. It's like going back in time, being in the Middle Ages and loving that experience.

St. Bernard dogs abound in the panorama. The people there ski all winter and get a lot of tourists every year. Aosta is a natural paradise. It is the best place to eat, ski and enjoy life. From Aosta to the west is France, and Switzerland to the north.

From the centre of Aosta, you should walk about 34 km to reach Monte Bianco and France and about the same distance to Switzerland.

Aostan people love sports and culture. They have excellent slopes where young people are prepared to compete in world ski championships; in fact, many world champions in skiing have come from Aosta. Another strength is athletics, such as walking, speed racing, gymnastics and many other athletic competitions.

Sound and the great Italian composers are a constant throughout the city. Also, the culture is always present in Aosta, the classical composers. Every year, there are several concerts by experts who play the folkloric music of Piedmont.

The Disalvatore family was beautiful, a typical Italian family.

Costantino's family was the Habsburg family, which was his surname. The Habsburgs were like the royal family. The

Habsburgs were untouchable and full of power. Wherever you could find their tentacles, they handled and influenced the system in a thousand ways. Five families were running the country. The Habsburgs were the fifth. It would be like in old England where the Yorks, Lancasters, Windsors, Wales and Wessexes were with the difference that this family's surname was Habsburg.

They were like the house of the Habsburgs who ruled Europe in their time and whose archduke Charles said that "the sun never set in our domain". Thus, the family of Costantino would be a version of that historic ancestral family, but in the twentieth century.

A family full of power, a father in the rockstar category because he was like the king of rock and the king of business, both at the same time. His father was loved like a rockstar, and he was famous in that same dimension. Costantino had a mother, three brothers and a sister. Among the brothers, some were more prominent than others. Perhaps the one with the most notoriety and exhibition was his father, Mr Adler Habsburg.

Adler means eagle and truly lived up to its meaning. He was the boss, as it would be popularly called "the boss", indicating that he was the big fish since he had the last word on matters concerning tangible things in the Habsburgs world.

Costantino worked in the bookstore, but it was like a hobby or for keeping himself busy. Perhaps, after all, that would be the problem, to have everything, to have so much that he forgets the important, and with so much free time, he may well feed the shadow.

The shadow has always ended up getting rid of everything, ruining everything and everyone's life.

Costantino was that typical man who could seduce all kinds of women because he was in the prince category. Still, he was not interested in women.

The dimensions for measuring a prince according to the system of this world are not the same measures that God uses to measure one. Of course, Allegria still did not know or understand that she should not look outside, that what matters is the heart, as God said to the prophet Samuel: "Do not consider his appearance or his height, for I have rejected him. The Lord does not look at the things people look at. People look at the outward appearance, but the Lord looks at the heart" (1 Samuel 16.7).

The Habsburg family were skiers; they ate in five-star restaurants above the Alps, had a luxurious lifestyle, and were fanatics of the organic lifestyle; they ate only food that had been processed without synthetic products.

The Habsburgs were owners of a Roman villa; the Roman Empire had built the house where they lived, and the walls were a historical monument; just by walking into that Roman villa where Costantino lived, you may feel transported to the time of the empire. They lived on Via Parigi Street in Aosta. The house was not so far from Allegria's home.

Although they lived in Aosta for commercial reasons, they were Germans, fanatics of their powerful Germany. Costantino's father had bought the villa to receive specific customers. The idea was to intimidate customers when they entered the place.

The Roman villa had its vineyard, producing delicious vintage wine. It had a swimming pool with a warm or temperate current of water and another swimming pool with a fresh breeze of water. The village had access to the forest, and there was a way to climb up to the Alps on the other side of the woods.

The cold water used in the house, coming down from the Alps current, was melted snow. The vast yard displayed all kinds of flowers, some of which were imported; there were also horses and antique car collections.

Everything in that house was huge and impressive. The windows were medieval stained glass windows, and the rooms had Roman frescoes depicting the daily life of the once most powerful Western empire.

In the courtyard, there was a large oven where every day, the baker prepared the Valdostano bread, focaccia, ciabatta and the fabulous grissini, something very typical of Turin and the Piedmont area.

The house chef cooked using only the animals raised in the corral and the herbs they grew in the inner patio. The chef used to prepare different dishes for lavish banquets. The food pantry had various collections of mushrooms and spices. Their barn had several cows, sheep, pigs and goats, and the Hapsburgs consumed only the best of their produce. The cooking oil was also made of olives from the olive trees in the same village.

With its columns and stairs, the floor was made of marble, the best marble obtained in Rome. The carpets that adorned the floor were made of medieval collection Isfahan silk, unique pieces impossible to get in the market.

They had a heating system where the stoves were carved out of stone, with ceramic stone from Aosta. They collected paintings. Bruno Amadio was one of the favourite painters of the family. His paintings had a particular highlight inside the town.

Bruno Amadio was also known as the "Cursed Painter". There is a black legend around him that says that his paintings attract misfortunes to those who own them. Perhaps this was another omen that would announce that trouble would knock on the door of this house, this superb villa. It is incredible, but some people have a splendid life but know how to open the doors to misfortune.

The villa's doors were made of the same timber as the Alps. They were carved and polished, they were handcrafted doors, and the central entrance had a Latin inscription: "Honesta mors turpi vita potior" - Tacitus, which translated into our language would be "Better an honourable death than a life without honour". That family even seemed to defend the values and be so honourable. Everything seemed perfect in that house. Of course, it just looked like being flawless; the reality was different. The fact was that hell was brewing from within. This villa had become a shrine of something twisted.

The Habsburgs had three families who worked daily to keep everything in the village in perfect condition.

At the entrance gate of the village, there was an arch made with mosaics which portrayed the image of Mary holding her baby child.

It was an amazing place, like all of Aosta.

Aosta is beautiful and flabbergasting. It has the third most beautiful castle in the world. Hence all its culture evokes history and beauty.

There was the great Costantino with his family. He seemed to be the perfect prince, and Allegria was amazed, mesmerised by this external glow.

Of course, Allegria was hypnotised by the external glow, by how gorgeous everything looked on the outside. She didn't stop to look at the heart. She didn't stop to look at the shadow in his heart because if she could see the shadow in Costantino, he would have stopped being a prince in the eyes of Allegria.

When someone is in their twenties don't care to go beyond what see and to analyse hearts and shadows. All of us in our twenties look only at the external things, the physical beauty, the charms, the warmth and the kindness of a person.

It can be subtle or deceptive if a person does something good and already seems reasonable to us without realising that many people do good but with bad intentions, which is a sin.

However, when someone is in their twenties, sin seems to be committed only by those who steal and kill. We do not read hearts and do not mind reading them. We want action, joy and love; sometimes, we must realise it to avoid looking for it in the wrong places.

Allegria needed more cleverness. At the time, she might have been aware that she should read hearts, not appearances, but she was enthralled by life and without so much experience that she had become easy prey to the hunter.

While Costantino belonged to the nobility, so to speak, he was a prince within the system; Allegria was not left behind and belonged to the true elite, for the Bible in Psalms teaches us that the true nobility is in those who obey God. True royalty is found among those who follow and keep the law of God; those are the true kings and queens.

Allegria obeyed God's commandments, and Costantino seemed to do so too, though deep down his heart was far from God, as Isaiah 29:13 describes it well: "These people come near to me with their mouth and honour me with their lips, but their hearts are far from me. Their worship of me is based on merely human rules they have been taught".

Some people look good if you see and hear them; everything looks like goodness on their lips, but you may wonder where their hearts dwell. "For where your treasure is, there your heart will be also" (Matthew 6:21), and honestly, Costantino had his heart in the shadow.

It's a pity that Allegria fails to see all this; unfortunately, at age twenty-one is oblivious to learning to read hearts. She didn't have the wisdom to read and understand hearts. She was fascinated with everything she seemed or looked good, the extraordinary things, everything that looked great; in fact, she just loved all those that looked deceptive.

For the moment, habemus romance! Who knows, maybe love will win.

***

The days passed, and Allegria decided to go with Laura to visit the bookstore and finally see the place where Costantino worked. The bookshop was next to the Valle d'Aosta Regional Library. Upon entering the bookstore, it seemed that peace and love abounded. Everything was clean, and the whole atmosphere was full of kindness.

Allegria smiled and grimaced to Laura. Then Allegria asked, "Are you sure we're in the right place?" Laura, a confident woman, looked at Allegria with a gesture meaning, "Girl, stop spinning around and go and say hello".

Allegria sighed, knowing she had to move forward to greet Costantino or drawback and listen to Laura's reprimands. It's a shame that Nicola and Marcella were not there at that moment. They would have understood; they would have been more merciful and patient.

Allegria thought that for the next time, if there were a next time, she would go with sweet Nicola, who didn't force her to talk or with the pragmatic Marcella, who talks all she wants and doesn't let anyone else speak; those friends would be better options than Laura. Anyway, she was there with Laura and drawing back was not a choice.

In the 90s, people wore waist jeans, planters, wide dresses and huge headbands, so Allegria, faithful to that style, wore flowery, loose clothing, like those dresses that don't have a hint of "hot" but a lot of sweet and maybe Allegria in that dress looked just like an angel. Costantino wore one of those vast T-shirts worn in the 90s, those basketball player T-shirts with rapper jeans and ADIDAS slippers. Remember, in the 90s everything was huge, especially clothes.

If it was about style, they were like each other, the two without a good style.

Allegria came over to say hello, thinking that maybe she'd listen in the background to "Ice, Ice Baby" (Vanilla Ice) or "The Rhythm of the Night, this is the Rhythm of my life" (Corona), even better if it had been playing "Hi Barbie, Hi Ken! Come on Barbie girl, let's go party!" (Acqua) because that would imply that he is Ken, she is Barbie; maybe some of those background music would have helped.

Still, nothing sounded in the background, just a silence that became more noticeable to the two faint-hearted new lovers.

Allegria tenderly says, "Hello!" and smiles. Costantino turns around and joyfully says, "Wow, hello, what a nice surprise! It's good to see you! That was a great show, wasn't it? All the music, from when the band appeared, how the stage exploded and us!". When he said 'us', that meant in Allegria's mind 'gosh', he said 'us!' that means she was included in the experience. She exclaimed, "Oh, yeah, it was fantastic!"

Costantino noticed that Allegria was blushing and slowed down, saying, "Well, I mean, the whole night was spectacular". Allegria nods and adds, "Yeah, it was an unforgettable night". Then silence invades the conversation between the two hearts.

Laura shakes her head and hands whispering, "Allegria, keep talking!". Allegria obeys Laura's order, looks at the books, takes anything off the shelf, and says, "Francine Rivers, she's an excellent writer! This novel was a best-selling one!" Costantino looks at the cover and explains how good writer Francine is and how successful she has been.

Allegria immediately reads a review that Rivers received for "A Voice in the Wind." Allegria was reading about this great author: "Rivers presents us with an ending that puzzles our emotions: Happiness, sadness, anger, joy and gratitude; a complete wave of feelings that cannot be defined individually -Allegria begins to play with her voice, giving different tonalities and making Costantino laugh- This reading takes us out of our comfort, makes us think about the freedom we enjoy and evaluate the intensity of our faith and convictions". Allegria sighs, returning to her normal voice and exclaims, "Interesting, what do you think of defending the faith, sacrificing comfort, freedom to defend the faith, along with conviction?"

Costantino nods and coldly replies, "Come on, Allegria, there is no need to defend the faith. We live in a Christian era. Everyone is a believer, you, me, everyone. We are in the age of comfort. There is no need to go to Calcutta to make sacrifices, Mother Teresa is already there". Allegria lifts her eyelashes and grimaces her lips, showing her disagreement. She was not in favour of what she was hearing.

Costantino's problem was that he loved the comfort; he didn't know about sacrifices and denying his flesh and instincts. After all, he had fed the shadow in the last years, and he didn't know what was it to receive a "no" for an answer; his life had never had many problems.

His life has been full of yes to this and that. It has always been yes to anything he wanted. That yes to everything would be the reason for his iniquity.

Sadly Allegria did not suspect that monstrosity; she could only see the light-filled side in which Costantino lived and made a living.

How could she not be attracted to Costantino when everything looked so perfect in his world? Everything was full of light and truth. Being in a space full of light and truth doesn't make you light and truth, but Allegria couldn't see that. Allegria only saw the perfection that radiated that environment and Costantino himself.

A wise adviser would ask Allegria, "Can't you understand that duality exists? That a person can look like one thing and be another, may think one thing and do something else". No, duality did not exist in Allegria's mind, for her sincerity dwells everywhere. She believed in an environment full of light and truth that seemed perfect.

Allegria puts the book in the display case, takes another one by Rivers, and reads it as "California... the gold rush, 1850. A time when men sold their souls for a bag of gold and women sold their bodies for a place to sleep". Allegria was surprised and thought, "- Phew, what a mad world! I just happened to read this now, but she kept reading as if she was unaware of what she was reading-. Angela expects nothing but betrayal from men. She was sold into prostitution as a child and survived by keeping the hatred that consumed her alive. What she hates the most are the men who use her, leaving her empty and dead inside. Then she meets Michael Hosea, a man who seeks to do his Father's will in everything. Michael obeys God's call to marry Angela and love her unconditionally. Slowly, day after day, he faces every bitter expectation of Angela until, despite her resistance, her heart, frozen with hatred, begins to melt away- from the novel 'Redeeming Love'".

Allegria smiles and adds, "Wow, I would have chosen another novel. It seems like very intense 'Redeeming Love'; I think the only redeeming love that is worthwhile is the love of God, who is daring to rescue us all; only Jesus saves us, and there are some who want to be rescued and others who refuse to do so. I don't know if it's worth loving people unconditionally". Costantino nods and says "That's a great truth, not everyone wants to be rescued". Allegria puts this second last book on the shelf and is ready to leave the place.

Costantino says, "We had a good talk. Will I see you again?" "Yes, maybe, I love books. I'll return. Edmundo De Amicis wrote "A house without books is a house without dignity". It's always good to read, bye-bye!". Costantino comes over, takes her hand, and whispers, "I think so, too. See you around Allegria!".

Allegria smiles with emotion, and Costantino looks expressively every second she is in the bookstore. Every time they glance at each other. They seem to feel the emotion that love produces: their dialogue, everything, absolutely everything, radiated love among themselves at the time.

Allegria went out with Laura from the bookstore. Allegria was so excited and delighted. Allegria loved all full of light, love, modesty and decency. She loved the world Edmundo De Amicis described in "Cuore", where all people are wise, good, caring and hardworking and where everybody loves their country and preserves their honour, wants to learn, values education and good manners, respect the rules and keep what is worthy as such. Perhaps Allegria was in love with this world, and Costantino seemed to emanate all this; he seemed to proceed similarly.

After all, Costantino was a Habsburg. Who could be better than a man who belonged to that royal world to behave like a prince? Perhaps the royal surname would help this prince to act as such, but as the saying goes, "appearances deceive", and duality was always a constant in Costantino's life.

He appeared perfect, royal, modest and even in love with good manners. Still, in reality, he only loved the shadow, which he had been feeding day after day, time after time, without realising that the shadow would someday grow and expand in such a way that would absorb him into itself so he would forget about what was good, worthy, honourable, along with good manners and ended up turning it into a monster, into a disfigured and even despicable being.

When does someone lose the North? When does someone decide to become disfigured? It is as if someone was born to succeed but decided to fail. Unbelievable. One cannot conceive of someone deciding to boycott himself. Sadly it is something that happens. The human being is a box full of surprises, and deep down, we never know how the heart and mind will lead us in that direction. The ways of the heart are unfathomable; who can describe them? Only God.

The romance is about to begin, and we don't want it to end before it begins, let's give them a chance. After all, love is always supposed to triumph.

***

Allegria and Laura talked about everything that happened in the bookstore. Both were so happy, like young girls who see love bloom.

They ran to the mall to have a snack and watch the match between Italy and Argentina, it was the 90s, and the World Cup was being played! No matter how much romance blooms, nothing can stop someone from going out and celebrating his roots.

Allegria was fascinated by enjoying good football in the World Cup, so this would be a match not to be missed. It was an exciting match because both teams were going 1-1. The teams would go to penalty kicks. It was a moment of tension. It could be heard the breathing of everyone in the shopping mall. Everyone was looking at what was going to happen. It was Italy's turn to score but Donadoni missed the penalty, and then Goycochea stopped Serena's last sentence. Argentinian went on to the final, and Italy was out of the World Cup.

"E'stata una notte triste"… very sad! Perhaps all the great stories begin this way, with the prince at the door and the young woman who awakens to the new season of life called: love. Maybe Allegria should have taken it as an omen, as an omen of what would come to her life would be sad. Very depressed and miserable. However, Costantino seemed the embodiment of kindness with a royal accent. What more could you ask for?

Sometimes events or situations show how everything will turn out or end. Like when you dream about something, but in the end, the dream will hurt the dreamer. Have you ever felt left out of something? Being an outcast but knowing that, in reality, it was your turn to play in the finals. However, you were taken out, you were eliminated in the preliminary round, and you didn't get to where you were supposed to. The things in life, the things in soccer, are similar sometimes.

Why take the omen of the "Argentina versus Italy" football match so severely if the World Cup was in Italy and Italy was still the central player in the World Cup, even though it was eliminated? Maybe like this story, it was everything in Allegria's life: to become the main character not because she had passed to the final but because the good or the bad decisions of Costantino would have to do with her, the last would continue to be played on her court, despite her emotions and she would see that final even though she had been knocked out.

It is incredible what God allows us to see because, after all, Allegria was a daughter of God, a daughter of light; she represented heaven. Heaven is always present despite the darkness. Light always shines amid the night.

The same day when she went to the bookstore, Italy lost the match and was out of the cup, a cup played in its own country; it was like a foreshadowing of what she would be living in her next years together with Costantino.

Allegria could not see what was coming. Maybe someone could have told her so that she could avoid so much pain.

Allegria radiated light, but the darkness approached her life. Each time she was closer to Costantino, the darkness increased.

Light is made of protons and is the only thing not destroyed. It is transformed. Despite Allegria's adversity, she will not be killed but be changed as light.

Allegria did not have a sensual beauty. She had a beauty that radiated light, a beauty that emanated wisdom. She was not someone sexually coveted. She was not sexually desirable, but she was attractive in other ways. Perhaps, that was attracting

Costantino, the soul of Allegria, who was light and belonged to heaven.

Aristotle said that "it is during our darkest moments that we must focus to see the light", and that would be about to come out in the life of Allegria, the greatest virtue.

Allegria, on her way home after the loss of the match in Italy, turns on her walkman and listens to the World Cup anthem on the radio: "Notti magiche, inseguendo un gol, sotto il cielo di un'estate italiana. E negli occhi tuoi, voglia di vincere. Un'estate, un'avventura in più. È un sogno che comincia da bambino, e che ti porta sempre più lontano. Non è una favola, e dagli spoglatoi, escono i ragazzi e siamo noi".

One magical night following a dream becomes increasingly distant. All that Allegria had experienced that day, a magical day, lived a vision of love and awakening to a new season. Still, she did not know what awaited her in that dream would become something awful, sad and undesirable.

Time will let us know how this story will end up. The night was splendid, even though Italy lost the match and was out of the World Cup. The night was extraordinary for celebrating life, football and love.

Allegria started planning when she could go back to the bookstore with Laura.

"The fate of many men depended on whether or not there was a library in their parents' house" (Edmundo De Amicis). If the future of Allegria depended on having books in her parent's house, the end of Allegria was guaranteed; her father taught her to love God and books.

Books were her second company. Heaven always was her first friend. God was her first choice, but the second one was the pages from front cover to back cover.

Allegria was returning to the bookstore to find her second company; "books".

Perhaps, she would find the one who replaces books in that bookstore, love? We'll see… they say that love can be just around the corner or around the bookstore.

***

Costantino was pleasantly impressed with Allegria; he thought she was the funniest and wittiest woman in the world. Costantino looked so perfect, like the ideal prince, but duality was always present.

The damned duality, to be one thing at times and something else at other times. Not only was there his duality, but the thing is also that it was constantly nourished.

It all began so excitedly by consuming pornography and sexual fantasies. Then these fantasies were not enough, and so this duality called perversion starts to increase more quietly, like when rats invade a house, at first, they are one or two rats. Still, not cleaning the home, rats reproduce and eventually populate every room and corner. Costantino seemed to control his duality. It looked as if it was under control and stable.

They say that every family has a weak link. It seemed that he would not be the weak link within the family, he even seemed to be one of the most vital links that could perpetuate the influence and the Habsburg dynasty, but no, frankly, Costantino was the weakest link, the one who appeared to love the good life but lived his life incorrectly. His duality would sooner or later explode because time shows what is in the heart, where he will write his life, whether in heaven or hell.

Costantino, the golden boy who had a beautiful childhood, loved by his parents, was born to succeed because all the paths in his life were destined to grow, get to the top, and be excellent in everything, but he had his choice. He has chosen the only path that would destroy him: the way of perversion.

According to the Bible, God defines some sins as abominations. Costantino chose that path, a terrible path.

Allegria didn't even know that this golden prince could have such a dark side, it was all so secret, subtle, and guarded that even just listening to that side of Costantino would surprise someone, and it would be hard to believe it.

Everything was as well kept as a state secret. They know what it's like to have someone you thought you knew next to you, but you never really knew him.

Having next to you a person who is never satisfied can hurt because he has already tried everything, and you will never be enough for that person. He has been through everything! Nothing on earth may surprise this person anymore.

Someone in that position has gone through the gates and beyond, down the subway of strange stairs and tasted what no one else has tasted: the dubious pleasures. Costantino was not used to refusing anything; he loved treats and to satisfy himself, so why not go down those strange stairs?

He didn't realise that by deciding to descend, he would begin to walk a tortuous, infinitely demonic path, and this would be like accessing the direct way to hell. When someone crosses the gates, it would be like choosing the path of loneliness and depression because that descent is when someone is lonely, and it is the time when there are no real friends.

The real problem is that Costantino pretends to be in the light, but in reality, he loves the darkness, he pretends to be on the path of light, but the fact is that he caresses the darkness in secret. Costantino was the weak link because he decided to be frail and embraced darkness instead of fighting it.

"For there is nothing hidden that will not be disclosed and nothing concealed that will not be known or brought into the open" (Luke 8.17), the hidden things would eventually come to light.

***

The romance between Allegria and Costantino started so tenderly, and it looks so pure and sweet with these two amazing youngsters. Let's keep the secret safeguarded in the dark and, even for a minute, believe that perhaps even the wicked darkness may be overcome.

Allegria only knew the light and knew nothing of darkness. She would never have imagined that such a golden and bright young man would lead her to the most incredible sadness ever.

Hold up, but let us not ruin Romeo and Juliet's romance before its time. Perhaps we cannot defy the omens. Maybe we cannot confront the prophecies. They say that "everything is possible", and Allegria believes that "everything was possible", but there are things that just cannot be, situations that cannot happen. You must not challenge God's destiny but humbly accept His will.

Thus, Allegria was convinced she was on the right side of the story. Everything could be possible for her. After all, she was from heaven. She belonged to heaven. How could there be an impossibility for her?

These two youngsters are just getting to know each other, and love is being born, let love guide them. If love indeed shows them, God will guide them. After all, "God is love".

Dawn came up. The sun rose bright and shining. The Alps looked astonishing in the panorama. People were brewing coffee for breakfast. Bakeries were already selling fresh bread. The street was noisy, with cars honking, people looking around, and others riding bicycles to work. The shops began to open their doors, people were on the road training and running, and two neighbours were fighting because one was hanging clothes on the balcony, and the clothes were covering the neighbour's patio. This kind of thing may happen only in Italy!

Allegria had to go to work. She worked in a clothing store that sold all kinds of women's garments; she was an excellent saleswoman. Milan was the city that had the most influence on her due to the whole world of fashion. She was skilled in serving customers and even used to sell clothes in bulk to the general public making such great deals. Besides studying history and philosophy at the University of Aosta, she liked to read and always raised many questions. In her spare time, she was always reading a book. She had an expressive and outgoing side but also a reserved one. She liked spending time with people but also wanted to isolate herself. Her creative and observant mind needed some silence from time to time.

Allegria ran the shop that belonged to a couple based in Milan, whose last name was Ferrara, so she was like the shop's general manager. This couple used to come to Aosta on Fridays to make the sales balances together with her.

It was the 1990s, so her speciality inside the store was the T-shirts gondola, that mountain of T-shirts that could be seen under a sign that read "Lady T-shirts". Once she arrived at the place, Allegria was ready to have coffee when Laura rushed to Allegria's job because she had an invitation for her. They had to go together to the next concert organised by the church!

Allegria smiled cheerfully. She had to go to the next concert and find something new to wear because Laura and Allegria were flirtatious. Although Allegria didn't have so much style, she liked to be very feminine when choosing her clothes, and if they were going to the concert, she had to be dazzling! It's all about love because love motivates someone to shine, so as the friends were very feminine, they would prepare for the concert in the best way, and fate would manage to keep the story going.

Laura will go with her boyfriend, Felipe. Like every cautious woman, she knew exactly how she had to look, a plaid dress to the body, flared in the skirt, as it was worn in the 90s.

Allegria would wear a newer style, a white blouse, a checked pleated skirt, and boots. Both ladies were faithful to femininity. Laura was the classic romantic girl, while Allegria was the typical innovator. Perhaps this is because Allegria was always looking for something more. She knew that this couldn't be everything, that an extraordinary future awaited her life and that she only had to make it happen. Allegria believed that she had to manage her destiny, that God had already given her everything she needed, talents and skills, and that she only had to develop those gifts.

Hence, Allegria did not sit down and watched life go by. She believed that she should influence and impact her life and become the architect of her story. Of course, as long as God had permitted her to build her own story.

A good artist should not be obsessed with being a pilot, and a good pilot should not be obsessed with being a cook; each one is wonderful within the gift and talent that God has given to each of them because our talent indicates that God gave us permission to shine or develop within that area.

God has a plan for us, and our talents speak out about that plan. That talent is inside you, and you need to make it shine. Allegria believed this truth, so she was constantly innovating.

The concert will be the following Friday. The excitement got higher throughout the week.

Laura and Felipe would pick up Allegria and go to the show together.

Felipe was a perfect boyfriend. He was stable and considerate of Laura's needs. He cared for Laura with such love that they looked like the ideal couple, everything a young woman would dream of.

Felipe was a hard-working young man studying engineering at the university and was, above all, a good Christian. He lived what he believed. He was not a troublemaker. He believed in God and made Him part of his life.

What was remarkable about Felipe was that he lived this truth: "And over all these virtues put on love, which binds them all together in perfect unity" (Colossians 3:14). That was his way of loving Laura. He always knew how to proceed with love towards her, being patient in listening to her, being considerate of her shortcomings and learning how to celebrate her joys with her.

Felipe had learned to love Laura in a perfect way. It is not easy to love that way, but when one is connected to the source of love, God, one has the strength and endurance to develop character and love that way. In short, Laura and Felipe were the perfect couple. Wherever they went, people were amazed by the love that united them.

It was Friday, the time came, and Felipe, Laura and Allegria were on their way to the concert.

Costantino was already in the concert auditorium. He was waiting could see the beautiful Allegria once again.

Chapter 2
"Remember tonight… for it is the beginning of always".
Dante Alighieri

Felipe, Laura and Allegria entered the concert hall, and everyone looked at them, maybe because they looked beautiful and in all the decades, being pretty makes someone attractive. If a girl is attractive, she's popular among boys. However, being popular just because a girl looks hot is not a substantial argument.

However, spiritual attraction exists; you can add intellectual appeal, a likeable character, and a pleasant personality, which generate genuine interest.

These qualities remain with them throughout a lifetime and endure despite the ups and downs of any relationship. Having a crush on someone seems to be a sensation when such beauty is seen, but the character makes that sensation last longer, and the true feelings are established.

They were just 20-year-old youngsters! What's wrong with being attractive? What problem can be there in attracting attention for being beautiful? They were not thinking in deep thought.

Being beautiful turns a woman attracting attention everywhere she goes, and guys admire hot girls, and they can set the trend.

If you decide to be a trend, make sure you are looked at and admired for the right reasons and that you are an influence to generate a much better world. Make your beauty, skills, and values affect others for good so you leave a better world than the one you have come into.

That truth was something that Allegria was very clear about. All the influence a person can have must be used for good.

Being a destructive influence for the wrong reasons in the wrong way, sooner or later, will end up killing the same person because apart from God, we can't do much good.

Separate from the influence of heaven, nothing good can be achieved.

Allegria knew that the essential was invisible to her eyes. Values and principles cannot be seen, but a life governed by admirable values can be observed.

Despite the disco-style lights, the concert was not great, and the audience was boring. It wasn't like the other concert where there was a fire. In this concert, there were only ashes, and the audience tried their best to answer the host band, but nothing happened. Nothing set the mood in the place; nothing could cheer the people up in that concert until… Allegria showed up, and he was there!

Costantino was at the concert, they both looked at each other and just smiled, he greeted everyone, shook hands with Felipe, kissed Laura on the cheek and did the same with Allegria, but when he kissed her, he stopped for a few more seconds as if he wanted to give her a long kiss.

Felipe and Laura observed and grimaced as if they were accomplices. Allegria, feeling followed by them, whispers to Costantino, without anyone else hearing: "You kiss me so holily". Costantino replies: "Oh yes? That's Shakespeare! Yes, in his novel Romeo and Juliet when they meet, when they first met, yes, it was just like when I met you!" Allegria smiles, blushing and decides to look at the stage for not making the moment so obvious among friends.

Although it seemed that Costantino wanted to love Allegria, the shadow always stopped him from going further.

Costantino dreamed of holding Allegria's hands. He wanted it badly, but the shadow always stopped him from loving her. Damn it! The damned shadow was destroying his life, and the worst part was that Costantino was secretly hugging and caressing the shadow. Why didn't he face the music? Why didn't he try to defeat it? But no, Costantino didn't have the strength of character to fight something. He was weak… weak inside, like a mentally disabled person who wants to walk, but deep inside his thoughts, he accepts his disability. He even begins to see the good side of that disability when his legs are perfectly capable of walking.

Costantino was fascinated by the beauty of Allegria, not only because of her external beauty but more than anything else because of her internal beauty. Everything that he had always dreamed of could be honest in a woman. Allegria was cheerful, smiling, happy, full of light and life, pure, virgin and with integrity.

Costantino saw Allegria as a saint, sublime, full of virtue! As Romeo exalted Juliet, "Oh, what a saint!" Costantino wanted to kiss those lips so severely, but he knew for that kind of purity he was so wicked because very deep in his heart, he caressed the shadow that would destroy him. He stroked a shadow that he did not want to let go of.

Costantino knew that if he came too close to Allegria, he could "desecrate such a divine altar", as Romeo exclaimed to his Juliet. Allegria transported God. She was an altar, a living sacrifice, and her life of integrity made the Holy Spirit dwell in her. Our bodies carry spirits. You decide which spirit you transport, some people carry lust, deceit, and lies, and others have agreed to transport God, love and mercy, making the body the temple of the Holy Spirit.

As the Bible says, "Do you not know that your bodies are temples of the Holy Spirit, who is in you, whom you have received from God? You are not your own" (1 Corinthians 6:19).

Allegria was so attractive in Costantino's eyes. Costantino was attracted to Allegria's light.

She was full of light because she had long decided a time to write her name in heaven, so all her good deeds reflected light and joy.

When she was very young, she heard the story of Jesus, who came to earth to love us, to die on the cross for our sins and rose again on the third day, thus overcoming Satan, the master of hell, corruption and the system of this world. Allegria had decided that she wanted to follow Jesus and that she wanted her name to be written in the heaven book.

From that day, the name of Allegria was recorded in heaven. Allegria was a faithful disciple of Jesus because she wanted to keep her name registered in heaven, as the Bible says, "that everyone who believes may have eternal life in Him (Jesus)" (John 3:15).

Costantino, however, inscribed his name in heaven from an early age. He had opted for Jesus as well, but he was not interested in keeping his name in the records of heaven; in fact, the shadow had become so attractive to him, the intense and wicked darkness, that everything concerning the forbidden had become his god, even though all that threatened to erase his name from the book of life, he did not care much for it.

All that was forbidden had become so secret and desirable to him that even though this shadow would drive him away from God and begin to open the gates of hell, he did not see all that as a threat because the shadow operated based on deception; Costantino was falling more into a scam.

Let's remember that deception is always presented in the most legitimate way possible but is not valid. It is the hook, and Satan, the master of lies, always disguises himself as an angel of light. It seems so desirable and promising what he presents to his prospects that someone would calmly consider it a great truth, a light. Still, once someone gets a bite of the forbidden fruit or simply goes into that light that turns out to be darkness, the soul begins to descend into hell.

***

Biting into the forbidden fruit is simply the gateway to hell. The more someone feeds his life on the forbidden fruit, the worse the hunger will become and slowly sink into eternal fire.

Unfortunately, Costantino was not wise enough to realise it. Folly is someone of Costantino's characteristics because he rejected correction towards his evil deeds, "Those who disregard discipline despite themselves, but the one who heeds correction gains understanding" (Proverbs 15:32).

Costantino has gradually been turning a deaf ear to discipline, laws, order, and righteousness, so his soul slowly moved away from heaven and closer to hell.

It's incredible; you don't wake up in hell overnight. The descent is always gradual, little by little, quietly, methodically... and comes the decline. Eventually, you discovered that you had already reached the bottom, deep in the abyss.

Each day the shadow competed against everything else in secret because it was the priority in the heart of Costantino. The apostle Paul wrote for a reason: "Therefore, my dear friends, as you have always obeyed-not only in my presence, but now much more in my absence-continue to work out your salvation with fear and trembling" (Philippians 2:12).

Costantino had the characteristics of a rebellious heart, obstinate and stubborn towards evil, willing not to hear and obey. As if he was living up to his name since Costantino means "man of firm ideas, a bit stubborn," and so he was, with firm but stubborn ideas, very foolish.

How beautiful is the obedient person! Obedient to authority, to order, to laws, to principles, but Costantino was disobedient. He only obeyed if he was constantly observed and controlled. Still, once the observation and control disappeared, he could be a rebellious and obtuse man, becoming possessed by the shadow.

The shadow, his damn shadow. It is as if the beauty that he could have in the light became such an atrocity under the shadow. Even though he lost everything, he was unwilling to stop caressing it.

It is as if someone is fully aware that taking poison kills, but is still so stubborn about taking that poison because is so thirsty. Instead of seeking pure water to quench one's thirst, someone goes to the nearest thing available; "poison" and takes it, fully aware that this kills.

Costantino was blind, deaf, foolish and with a poor, naked soul. Costantino appeared as part of heaven but slowly opened the door to hell. He was lukewarm, and that would be his fate. "So, because you are lukewarm-neither hot nor cold-I am about to spit you out of my mouth. You say, 'I am rich; I have acquired wealth and do not need a thing'. But you do not realize that you are wretched, pitiful, poor, blind and naked. I counsel you to buy from me gold refined in the fire, so you can become rich, and white clothes to wear, so can cover your shameful nakedness; and salve to put on your eyes, so you can see" (Revelation 3:16-18).

Allegria has always worn white clothes; you could see; from Costantino, you could not. She might wish she'd known this before so she wouldn't have started this infernal journey! But no, she could only see the light-filled side of Costantino. She could only see one side, not realising that there was a dark side. She was just seeing one side of the coin.

They say that everything happens for a reason. Maybe the reason was that when they found each other, they could save each other. She could light up his world so that he would stop caressing the darkness, and he could save her from loneliness. That isn't a fact, though. Perhaps it was a chance, fate or tragedy.

Charles Chaplin said, "Time is the best actor... always finds a perfect ending". Let time figure out this puzzle, what awaits this young and inexperienced couple.

Despite the perversion invading Costantino's life, he still dreamed of holding Allegria's hand. Costantino thought that as a person with lights and shadows, he could still have a chance to tickle her hand.

Costantino had by then conditioned his heart on increasing the shadow within himself; however, when Costantino saw Allegria, he thought if he could have the good fortune to desecrate such a divine altar, as Romeo said to Juliet in Shakespeare's work, "If I have desecrated such a divine altar with my hand, forgive me. My mouth will erase the stain, like a blushing pilgrim, with a kiss". Costantino wanted to take Allegria's hand and longed to kiss her red lips.

Costantino took some courage at last, and in the middle of the concert, he took Allegria's hand, he blushed, and she smiled at him. They were both joyful. He doesn't let go of her hand, she looks at him, and it's as if she could read in his eyes the phrase, "Don't let me go, please don't ever let me go".

Perhaps it was a cry for help as if to say, "Don't you see that if you let me go, the shadow will swallow me up, the shadow will absorb me, and I may never come out again".

At that moment and in the middle of the concert, she could not understand the seriousness of the matter. She just knew that she should not let him go.

When he finally caressed her hand, and everything dispelled, there was no light, no darkness, just love, while light and darkness watched.

Costantino whispers to Allegria: "Listen to me calmly while my lips pray, and yours purify me" She replies, "Oh Romeo, I think I don't have the power to truly purify you" "How well she mocks the pain of others. Who never felt pain? If you understood my shadows, but what light appears there? Is the sun already rising from the balconies of the east? Rise and shine, beautiful sun, and kill the moon with your rays of envy, which is pale and haggard because it defeats your beauty to any nymph of your choir. You do not see how you shine my life with your soul as my sun, beautiful Allegria!".

She listens to him, absorbed and then shyly replies: "Really, Costantino?" "She spoke. I feel her voice again, Angel of love that you appear to me in the middle of the night!" "Costantino, I think you're a big fan of Shakespeare!" "I think I'm a big fan of love, making your love mine, Allegria!" They both smile, and he kisses her hand.

***

Felipe and Laura interrupted, saying that the concert was boring and that it would be better to go for something to eat somewhere. Felipe and Laura may have found the show tedious. Still, for Allegria and Costantino, the concert had been the most exciting thing they had ever experienced up to that point.

In the darks of the show, Costantino takes the opportunity to caress Allegria's hand for the last time without anyone noticing it.

Felipe insists, "C'mon, let's go, guys!".

They walk out to "Domino's Pizza" a famous pizzeria that started in the 1960s but was already a success by the 1990s. This pizzeria had more than a hundred stores nationwide and had become the most popular place for everyone in the decade. It was an inexpensive place to eat, where they offered one of the best pizzas, where all the youth would enjoy the mozzarella pizzas.

From that night, Costantino was in love with Allegria despite the shadow, and it was official, even though the darkness had taken root in his heart. Costantino couldn't stop loving Allegria. He bravely began to conquer this gorgeous girl.

In the 90s, no social network apps such as WhatsApp, Facebook or Instagram existed. The method was mail on hand, so he found out exactly where Allegria lived and started delivering letters to her, one or two per week.

Chapter 3
"From a little spark may burst a flame"
Dante Alighieri

Costantino used his old black Specialized bike; these bicycles were the most popular in the media as they monopolised most of the market with their spots and excellent prices.

Before going to work, Costantino would leave a letter in Allegria's mailbox, and since Costantino was not very good with words, he would copy some of the classic poems he thought described her by hand. The Disalvatore family mailbox kept getting letters that would read like this:

Allegria:

"Bella, as in the fresh stone of the spring, the water opens a wide flash of foam, so is the smile on your face, beautiful.

Beautiful, with a copper nest tangled on your head, a nest the colour of gloomy honey where my heart burns and rests fair. (Bella, Pablo Neruda).

Your smile lights up my day; you're all beautiful".

Costantino

(August 7, 1990)

Perhaps one of the things Costantino loved most about Allegria was her smile. Allegria's smile took away the darkness that had been consuming him, dispelled the night and even gave hope to his life that he might come out of the night. Well, what a dream, an idea to escape the night!

A few days later, Costantino repeated the same action.

Allegria:

"Because I have you and I don't, because I think about you, because the night is wide-eyed, because the night passes and I say, love, because you have come to reclaim your image, and you are better than all your images because you are beautiful from foot to soul because you are good from soul to me because you hide sweet in pride, small and sweet, armoured heart.

Because you are mine, because you aren't mine, because I look at you and die, and worse than dying, is not seeing you love, not seeing you.

Perhaps that poem was the sweetest and the bitterest one at the same time because it spoke of the deep love he was beginning to feel for her, but at the same time, with the silent growth of the shadow over his life; it was like an omen that they could not get to be together.

That poem reflected the saddest verse in history, like saying, "I am almost free to love you, but I can't". There is no word more painful in the dictionary than "almost", such as I almost had you, I almost could do it, I almost made it, I almost gave myself up... but somehow I failed to do so. It was like loving, longing and not having, not being able to.

It hurts to love her. Of course, it does hurt, but shouldn't one love until it hurts? The pain was sharp for both, as was the intensity, passion and strength. At the age of 20, you feel invincible. You dare to fight against hell and defeat it; what an idea! To beat hell, you need the help of heaven. Only heaven can beat it. Nonetheless, sometimes heaven doesn't want to help to overcome that hell that dwells in someone's life because that battle is for that person to fight. That person first had to decide to belong to heaven so that the whole of heaven could help him.

Why would Allegria fight that battle if Costantino rejects the fact of being saved?

Costantino secretly loved Allegria, who belonged to heaven, but more intimately, he loved hell, and there was within his heart a gigantic battle for who would win, whether Allegria, who represented heaven or the shadow, who represented hell.

***

Despite the increasing darkness in his life and the shadow that rules it, Costantino did not give up and kept thinking that one day he could be free, so he continued to give hope to Allegria, dreaming that one day they would be able to be together, united forever.

So driven by that dream, he wrote another letter.

Allegria:

"Like a bird flying clear across the air, I feel your thinking coming toward me and here in my heart, it's building its nest. My soul flowers open; the stems tremble like the fresh lips of a youth's first embrace of a beauty, the leaves stab like a knife as jealously bitter as the servants of a lady of the wealthy classes while busy preparing her marriage bed. My heart is large and it belongs to you. All of the sadness can fit inside my soul as long as the world cries, suffers, and dies!

With the dry leaves, dust, and fallen branches. I clean and carefully brush each leaf's brush; I take the eaten petals from the worms. I trim the lawn and look what I have found. See how your bird is now shrinking my heart! (Tree of my soul, José Martí).

In my thoughts, I always find you. I find your beauty and freshness, and I embrace you as if it were the first time I could embrace such beauty. My heart is wide but small for you when you come to me; my heart is tiny to hold you because of such immenseness you mean to me".

Costantino (17 August 1990).

Allegria was immense to Costantino, not because she was great in herself, but rather when a person is trapped in darkness, it is like being in a bottomless pit of darkness in the subsoil of hell while she was at the apex of heaven. How inconceivable is it that Allegria would want to go inside hell for being next to Costantino? Darkness always leaves people at a disadvantage. Being part of hell is like dwelling in this universe with all the possible weaknesses. It's like becoming a negative number because darkness ties you to the bottom of the abyss, while a person connected to heaven can only be a positive number. If you belong to heaven, heaven places you on the very top where you belong. To unite these two lovers would be like joining hell together with heaven. They were not congenial.

Costantino thought Allegria was attractive because she knew how to dress in the garment that made her impossible: "love". She knew how to follow this principle "And over all these virtues put on love, which binds them all together in perfect unity" (Colossians 3:14). She was beautiful because she dressed up with love.

God is love, so every day walking with God and demonstrating love to others is in so many ways "unique". How can we compete against that? There's no way because love will always prevail.

Allegria was becoming more beautiful daily because of love, and Costantino was becoming more damaged because of the shadow.

The shadow always appeared to whisper to him: "Why do you, the king's son, look so haggard morning after morning? Won't you tell me?" (2 Samuel 13:4). It was as if the shadow were saying to him: "How can you refuse yourself any pleasure, you are a prince! If abstinence from pleasure makes you sad, it is unjust because you deserve everything, all the satisfaction you desire!

That was the inner battle in Costantino's heart every day, but he tried humanely to silence that voice generated by the shadow because he wanted his love for Allegria to be stronger. He would try, but this may not last long. Sooner or later, Costantino would give up against the shadow.

In those days, Allegria was shuddering at the sight of such a profession of love, she was moved, and so it was that love for Costantino grew daily. She was puzzled, trying to understand why Costantino used to leave the letters and then disappeared. Couldn't he stay by her side? Couldn't he take some time to talk to her? Or take some time to see her when delivering his letters?

That's what she wanted, but it was something he didn't do. There were just letters, one after another, but he was never talking.

****

One day Allegria picks up her bicycle. That typical white bicycle with details of little flowers and a basket. She decides to go to Costantino's workplace. This time she had prepared a letter. She enters the bookstore where Costantino works, greets him, kisses him on both cheeks and leaves the envelope in his hands, after a little chatting. Costantino blushes and she quickly goes out. She left that place with a mix of happiness and shyness.

Costantino opens the envelope and finds the sweetest love letter.
Costantino:

"Stop, the shadow of my elusive beloved, image of enchantment that I most desire, a beautiful illusion for whom I happily die, sweet fiction for whom I painfully live.

If to the magnet of your graces, attractive, my breast serves as obedient steel, why do you capture my love in such pleasure, if you are to leave me later, fugitive?

But you cannot boast, satisfied, that your tyranny triumphs over me, for though you have eluded the tight noose, that encircled your fantastic form, it matters little to deceive arms and breast, if I fashion a prison for you in my fantasy. (Stop, the shadow of my elusive beloved, Sor Juana Inés De La Cruz).

You show up, and you don't stay. I miss you, but I only see your cards. I only see your shadow".

Allegria (August 24, 1990)

Allegria was sweet, and without wanting in her letter, she said the truth: "I only see your shadow", because Allegria did not understand that she was competing with the shadow, that the shadow was growing in Costantino and it was gradually absorbing him.

Costantino resisted the shadow. He tried to counteract the shadow instead of accepting it and refused to give in because deep in his heart, he truly wanted to be with Allegria.

Soothe her feelings and make her understand that his love was sincere, a few days later, he delivered the following letter.

Allegria:

"O flame of living love, that dost eternally, pierce through my soul with so consuming heat, since there's no help above, make thou an end of me, and break the bond of this encounter sweet.

O burn that burns to heal! O more than pleasant wound! And o soft hand, o touch most delicate, that dost new life reveal, that dost in grace abound, and, slaying, dost from death to life translate!

O lamps of fire that shined with so intense a light, that those deep caverns where the senses live, which were obscure and blind, now with strange glories bright, both heat and light to his beloved give!

With how benign intent rememberest thou my breast, where thou alone abidest secretly; and in thy sweet ascent, with glory and

good possessed, how delicately thou teachest love to me! (O Flame of Living Love, San Juan de la Cruz).
You are enthusiastic yet so tender that your life's flame sweetly makes me hopelessly in love with you. You set me free from my shadow. You give eternal bliss. Before you came into my life, I have been so dark and blind, absorbed by so many shadows, but you have sweetly made it through and dwell in my heart, where you have been all this time and where there's only room for you".
Costantino (August 28, 1990)

***

Allegria sighed with each of these letters. She was deeply moved. She could only love him back in response to so much love that she was receiving. She had no idea of the darkness she would face in deciding to love him, so she let her feelings flow and grow.

Facing such great love, Allegria took some paper and pencil and wrote one last letter, telling him it was the right time and that they should be together.

Costantino:

"If you love me, love me whole, not by zones of light or shadow... if you love me, love me black, and white, and grey and green and blond, and mixed... love my day, love my night... and in the morning with the open window!
If you love me, don't break me in pieces: love me whole... or do not love me at all. (Love me whole, Dulce María Loynaz)
I think it's time to sit down, have coffee and talk; love, be together."
Allegria (August 29, 1990)

It was time to see each other and to be together, entirely together, to walk holding hands, smile at each other, kiss, play... do everything that girlfriends and boyfriends do. So since the love between the two was so evident, he decided to write one last letter to her, where he would ask her out to start a relationship full of happiness and love.

Allegria:

"You come to me, you come near and announce yourself with such a light murmur, that you do not disturb my repose. You do not disturb, and it is a miraculous song each of the phrases you utter.

You come to me, you do not tremble, you do not waver, and there is such a strong attraction in looking at us that we forget everything, life and death, suspended in the light of your pupils.

And you penetrate my life and I feel you so close to my own thought and there is in possession so deep calm, that I interrogate the mystery in which I am fascinated if we are two reflections of the same being, the double incarnation of a single soul. (You come to me, Enrique González Martínez).

You come to me, and all these feelings spark in me. Our attraction is so strong that you absorb my entire centre. You don't tremble. You don't hesitate, while I do shudder. I think it's time for us to go cycling, have a snack together and talk about our love. I'll be waiting for you tomorrow at 4 pm in Piazza Manzetti, opposite the railway station".

Love,

Costantino (30 August 1990)

***

The Piazza Manzetti is one of the main places of Aosta, where all the people gather. It is where they usually hold fairs, and schools from other cities visit the site because it is a historical centre because of the relics of the Roman Empire that ornament the place. All the buses leave from that piazza. Even several cyclists gather there to go out and visit Aosta. This square joins the whole city, which makes it a significant central place.

Aosta is a beautiful city surrounded by the Alps, where one can breathe peace and clean air. It is a unique place in wonderful Italy. People are dynamic, cheerful, talkative and feel a lot of empathy. The sun even seems to smile in Aosta.

The city is a little remote and has a lot of crowds during the winter when people from all over the world go skiing in the magnificent and stunning Alps. August was a summery month, so not so many people were in attendance. Piazza Manzetti was the perfect place to let love flow.

Costantino had taken the step. He had done it at last. The date was set; August 31, 1990, would be an excellent day for both of them, love had visited them, and this feeling was there to stay.

They wouldn't pass up this opportunity. It would be a heavenly visit, as when heaven visits earth in love. Love had touched them and decided to unite them. Wow, what a feeling, what a sensation when the sky sees the world, as when love invades us. When tenderness and sweetness knock on our door!

It is the feeling called love. When love visits our lives, we experience a piece of heaven. In heaven, the only language spoken is love.

The day came, and the two youngsters met and started riding bikes, smiling and looking at each other... they loved each other. Suddenly they stop the bikes, and sit on the grass, and she says, "What huge trees, what immense forest" Costantino replies: "They are not more immense than you, no more immense than the black gaze from your eyes, no more immense than our love". Allegria, awed, replies: "Is it true? Do you love me? Won't you play with my feelings and then leave me?".

She was very insecure. She had seen so many disappointments in life that it was hard for her to believe that something good would happen to her because her whole environment had been full of deep sadness and dismay.

Even though she was not sad, she was an extremely optimistic and cheerful woman, her life sparked happiness, but the environment was bitter, gloomy and monotonous. It seemed that nothing good would happen until he appeared, this love, and she did not know whether it was real or just part of her dreams.

Understanding her fears, Costantino holds her hands and says, "Oh your hands laden with roses! Your hands are purer than roses. And among the white leaves, they emerge like pieces of stars, like the wings of white butterflies, like candid silks.

Did they fall from the moon? did they play in a celestial spring? are they soulful? They have the vague splendour of lilies from another world; They dazzle what they dream, and refresh what they sing.

My forehead is serene, like an evening sky, when you, like your hands, walk among its clouds; if I kiss them, the purple ember of my mouth Pales from its water-stone whiteness.

Your hands among dreams! They cross, doves of white fire, through my bad nightmares, and, at dawn, they open to me, as they are light from you, the soft clarity of the silver east".

Costantino kisses Allegria with sweetness and says "Allegria, you're too good to me, you bring calm and peace to my soul".
Allegria replies, "Well, it is worth quoting Shakespeare when you are doing a work of charity" Costantino is surprised and replies, "Allegria, it is not for my charity to love you; it is a delight, a sweet delight" Allegria, awed with tenderness, replies "Oh, thank you, Costantino, thank you for being so good!". She is surprised by the devotion of so much love that she says, "You have turned out to be a poet!" Costantino just replies, "Well, those phrases are not mine; I was using the words of Juan Ramón Jiménez, I like to read poems, and I always remember those that have something to do with my reality".
He holds her hands tightly and kisses her. She responds to that kiss, and tenderness and passion surround them. Love has come to them. It was calm, sweet, intense, passionate, everything, feeling everything in one afternoon.
After a few hours, they decide to return. Costantino accompanies Allegria to her door. They kiss goodbye at the doorway of the Disalvatore. She was flying. She had felt so much and so little… so little had been the time.
Upon arriving home, she greeted her parents with a kiss, and she was delighted. She has dinner and runs to her room to review the afternoon she had lived. Thank God for being benefited by such a great thing named love.
Then she went to bed. She returned to her routine the next day, but her life was no longer the same. Love and joy flooded everything she did.
She continued working and studying as usual. They were in love and happy.

Chapter 4
**"The darkest places in hell are reserved for those who maintain
their neutrality in times of moral crisis".**
Dante Alighieri

They had begun a tender and beautiful courtship. They meet as often as they can. Sometimes once a day. Other times they had to wait a few days to get together because of the activities at work or college.

They had agreed to have a date to celebrate their love since they had been dating for a month. Costantino planned to go for a walk together. He was waiting for her at six P.M. in the ruins of the Roman Empire where the Roman theatre was located, next to the conservatory of the "Istituto Musicale Pareggiato della Valle D'Aosta".

They would take a walk through the ancient Roman amphitheatre. How exciting! Aosta had hundreds of historical sites, and they were all extraordinary.

Allegria goes on a date with a simple white summer dress. Costantino was waiting for her with a bouquet. Costantino smiles with love when he sees her, and Allegria does the same thing. Each of them had that feeling one experiences when being head over heels in love.

Love makes us feel that the world seems beautiful and makes us smile unintentionally when that wonderful person is around.

Costantino approaches first, with his hands around Allegria's waist, and kisses her; she responds to the kiss, and they begin to walk together, holding hands. Allegria carried the small bouquet and was delighted with such a lovely surprise.

They were celebrating their first month together with a romantic picnic and seeing them walking together under the sunset along the ancient empire's walls. It was so tender. For the moment, they stopped at a place where Costantino had prepared a picnic. He had brought the coffee in a thermos flask and cookies with chocolate chips to celebrate that tender-hearted moment they were living together.

Then they began to tour the place and entered an old beautiful Roman house from ancient times. Allegria told Costantino that she knew about this house because they had studied the city's archaeological remains. She knew it belonged to a wealthy and prestigious family of patricians. They had been Christian.

In that house, all the walls had frescoes that told a story. Each column was made of marble brought from Rome, and each had a different design carved as each column told the story of Christianity.

Costantino is pleasantly surprised and continues to listen to her. She shows him one by one the different marble columns.

Allegria shows him the columns one by one and says, "This column tells the story of the flood; this one shows us Abraham coming out of his tent to tell the stars. Here we have Joseph ruling Egypt and saving the people of Israel from starvation. In this other column, we see Moses when the Red Sea opens. Here we have a beautiful love story; Boaz and Ruth; in this other column, we have David and Goliath, and in this other, Daniel in the den of lions. This other one is a little difficult to decipher; I think it is the prophet Ezekiel prophesying on the dry bones".

They keep walking, and Allegria shows him the four most beautiful columns.

These columns were in the main section to access the garden of the house, it was a place of honour, and she commented, "This column tells us the birth of Jesus in the manger, this one when Jesus calms the storm, this other column tells us about the miracle to feed more than five thousand people; and finally the most important of all, a column that supports the entire construction of the house tells us the story of the death of Christ along with his resurrection, see, here is the empty tomb! Four columns to tell us the gospel story. Why four? Because four means balance and perfection. It can be seen that whoever built this relic knew what he was doing because these three columns lead us to the central column: three is the number of the trinity, and four is the number of perfection. This work made him a true connoisseur of the subject".

While Allegria was narrating all this, she was fascinated by it. Costantino was wise enough to realise how good she was at talking about history but even more at talking about Jesus.

They continued walking and left the Roman house to pass through the arena. Suddenly, he surprised her, took her by the waist, raised her with his arms and kissed her passionately. It wasn't just any kiss. It was a secret kiss as if they were hiding from the rest. Nobody saw them, and they were experiencing so much emotion. It was those passionate kisses that couples usually give each other when they live a great moment of love together, wrapped in passion.

The world had stopped, the noise did not exist, and all good things had emerged; pure love.

There's no such delight in life as kissing in the ruins of the Roman amphitheatre or the sadness of kissing there if that person will not be your "forever".

Was all this experience love or just a play? Was the shadow more potent than any love that Costantino could experience? Well, time will let us know the facts. At that moment, everything seemed to indicate that all that experience was true love and that this great love would overcome darkness.

After such an extraordinary afternoon, they had to return to their homes. Costantino takes Allegria home and kisses her again. They were happy. They were beautiful. Together they made the perfect couple. They were meant for each other. They were blessed.

***

The question would be: will they last together? Because, like every couple, everything is excellent at first, but then problems arise to test or destroy the romance.

Time passed, and they began to experience different emotions because life is cyclical, and every person in their daily lives has ups and downs.

Costantino had some excellent qualities. However, he had one big flaw. He was a possessive, jealous person for no reason. He loved Allegria, but he wanted her all to himself. One part wasn't enough for him; he wanted everything; that may sound appealing, but it tends to suffocate over time. He wanted to be the centre of her. He wanted all of her. This kept her from doing anything to upset him. She avoided dealing with people or environments with whom he might feel insecure.

One day Costantino visits Allegria at her workplace, she receives him with a big smile, and they have some delicious hamburgers together. When they go out, they kiss passionately as usual, and he leaves her a note saying she should be only his and no one else's.
Allegria:
"Mine: that's your name.
What more harmony?
Mine: daylight;
mine: roses, flames.
What a scent you pour
on my soul
if I know you love me!
Oh, Mine! Oh, Mine!
I am sad, you're sad...
Will you not then be
mine till death? (Mine, Rubén Darío)
Allegria, I want you to be mine to the end of our days on earth".
Costantino
What a note! She had a hint of love but, at the same time, an indication of death because it was like he was demanding her whole life. At the same time, true love gives everything and does not take away anything. It was perhaps a harbinger of all to come: death, shadow, and darkness. We know she was very much in love and understood the message that she should love and respect him in everything. So because she was blinded by love, she did that; she loved and respected him in everything.

As their love increased, visit after visit, day after day, letter after letter, and kiss after kiss, the shadow subtly appeared, and darkness began to show slightly.

This was something that Allegria did not know, and even if she had known, it is something that she could not have avoided because no human being can overcome darkness and destructive forces. Only God could defeat all kinds of shadows. Only heaven can overcome darkness. Allegria was allied to heaven but did not have the strength to overcome what was coming.

***

Allegria loved God, and she had decided not to contaminate herself with the "food" and "drink" of the king of this world. She was not in favour of the system of this world. She built her life in a completely another system. "Heaven's system, Heaven's Kingdom".

The "food" spiritually talking represents the demonic doctrine that operates in the world, and the "drinking" means the evil spirits that work to control this world. It is how the system of this world works. This world likes its people. They don't like holy people. The saint people are out of the system.

Allegria admired the prophet Daniel and always remembered how Daniel lived his life. His example inspired her. "But Daniel resolved not to defile himself with the royal food and wine, and he asked the chief official for permission not to defile himself this way. Now God had caused the official to show favour and compassion to Daniel" (Daniel 1.8-9).

That was Daniel's secret, and Allegria knew this and applied it. Maybe that was why she had grace in the eyes of others because she was so different, and in that different way, she learned to find answers for her own. She learned to think differently, which made her strong. She was only associated with heaven. Just as the prophet Daniel in biblical times did not defile himself with what the king of Babylon offered but instead assigned himself to drink water and eat only vegetables and legumes, Allegria was determined not to become contaminated with everything this system provided.

What does the system offer? All kinds of pleasures, everything that is attractive to the senses. The devil knows how to charm the souls. He knows how to destroy the heart. To destroy everything pure and noble that you have. He offers you all the delicacies in such an appealing way that it is humanly impossible to refuse. He gives you everything you dream of. Pleasure, fame, popularity, a predominant place on the social scale, money, power, praises, building your empire within Babylon but without God, a complete exaltation of your ego, of your person.

The system of this world offers you hell, but it does not tell you it is hell because looks so inviting and attractive that you would never say it's a cell, but it is a prison cell. You became a slave of your sins. Babylon knows how to hunt you. It is so pleasing to your senses, before your eyes, touch, ears, smell and taste, that the logical questions arise: How to refuse? How could all these be ever bad?

Babylon doesn't tell you that it will give you anything but will take everything away. Babylon will give you everything you can imagine in exchange for your eternal soul. Babylon gradually gives you everything, but it destroys your soul, piece by piece, little by little, part by part, until you have nothing and can no longer choose what sin to commit or where to be. Ultimately, you must be satisfied with the leftovers that Great Babylon wants to offer you.

The system of this world, Great Babylon, is attractive, imperial, full of artificial lights, splendours that conquer your senses, hurtful, gloomy, and putrid simultaneously because sin always ends up bitter, painful, difficult and destructive. Babylon is made to hunt the soul. It is like an artificial light; by following it or catching it, you realise that it is not light but darkness, deep and dense darkness where demons and torments become the daily company of those who consume such light.

Allegria was intelligent and wise about this. However, Costantino wasn't. Allegria understood how this world was running. Costantino was unwise, not because he lacked liveliness, but because his foolishness was rooted in his heart, where the shadow caressed. He was trying to get out of the shadow, but at the same time, he was cultivating it. It was like a love-hate relationship. Sometimes he loved the shadow and moved away from Allegria. Sometimes, he hated it and approached Allegria.

Babylon is a system plagued with evil, immorality, perversion, hatred, resentment, competition, and lust. Its effects have a putrid smell even though they use French perfume to cover their wounds, to hide the scars. Babylon operated in the heart of Costantino, and Babylon continues to work throughout this world.

Babylon loves to manifest itself in the high places and sell you the image that they did it, that they are perfect, no matter how many people had to prostitute themselves on the way to the top. Because they don't show you the background, they show you the image of success. They don't tell you about the scars. They only show you the false glory because the day they stop serving in that empire, the empire of Babylon is in charge of finishing and eradicating them.

Allegria did not love Babylon. Indeed, she even despised that whole system she considered so false and prostituted. Allegria loved the law of Jehovah because she knew and understood that Jehovah's law is perfect and nurtures the soul. She preferred to accomplish little but to achieve it with dignity and to have a life in order. She loved to do things correctly, follow the rules, and not take shortcuts because she knew that taking shortcuts, crooked paths and slips would only involve pain and regret in the long run. She didn't want to accomplish anything in her life in a wicked way. She was determined to keep herself away from prostituting with Great Babylon. Nor does Costantino. Costantino was deeply attracted to everything Babylon offered, especially the pleasures. Pleasures without scruples.

***

How would someone think something wrong about Costantino since he worked in a Christian bookstore in Aosta and even looked like an angelic boy?
Maybe that's why Costantino was attracted to Allegria, because he was attracted to her purity, that she was intact when he was dirty, with a huge shadow, with so many wrong thoughts in his soul. Costantino had the perfect image of outer life, while his inner self was rotten, Allegria may not have been perfect in terms of her outer self, but her inner self was excellent, healthy, and pure. It was a pity Allegria couldn't understand the smell of Costantino's soul.
Allegria, as she was pure, thought others would respond with the same goodness.
Sometimes you can give much good and only receive evil, although God will ultimately help you to reap the good you sowed.
Costantino held Allegria's hands and kissed her. He felt he was touching the sky with his hands and lips. However, Costantino, with his soul, touched hell, night after night, secretly caressing the shadow. He admired heaven, but in his heart, he loved hell.
The nature of Costantino was like the heart of King Solomon. "Solomon did wrong before God and did not obey him; in fact, he never promised to obey him completely, as his father David had done... he never obeyed Him" (1 King 11). So was Costantino. He

never really obeyed God. He sincerely never wanted to follow the greatest kingdom, the empire that remains forever, "the kingdom of heaven".

Honestly, Babylon was beautiful to him, so seductive that he could not mitigate in his mind the charms of that false and cruel empire called Babylon, the great harlot. The great whore who diverts those who follow good to turn them to evil.

Costantino wanted to love Allegria, but first, he had to leave the shadows altogether. Then he came up with a plan. He would make a journey to overcome the shadow entirely because he knew that he could not love Allegria just partly. He had to love her completely, in her whole dimensions, as she deserved.

He takes courage in one of his casual datings to have a snack or ride a bicycle, between poems and caresses, kisses and smiles. He tells her that these three months were the three most beautiful months of his life but that he needed to make a trip to overcome things and solve problems, but that before Christmas, he would come back for her. She nods and understands that they were very young and that perhaps some issues needed to be solved before embarking on the adventure of living forever together, that great love that united them. That was his farewell evening. They were not sad. They were hopeful, and they knew they would see each other again. They knew they would soon be together as they had hoped.

Costantino can't help but break some tears and says to Allegria: "You are my life. You must know that you are my life!". She smiles in disbelief but doesn't want to discuss it and says, "Sweetie, you are my life too". They hug and kiss. They love each other. Despite the shadow, they both loved each other immensely. We would only have to know if this love was more substantial than the shadow.

Costantino accompanies her to the house, and before saying goodbye, he gives her the last letter, asks her to open it when he has left for Germany the next day, and asks her not to go and say goodbye because all that would make it more difficult. She gives her word that she will not say goodbye. The next day Costantino took the plane to Germany to work in another bookstore branch in Frankfurt.

Tears roll down sadly as Allegria opens the last letter he left her and starts to read:

Allegria:

"While I kiss you, its murmur gives us the tree that rocks to the sun the gold, that the sun gives it as it flees, the fleeting treasure of the tree that is the tree of my love.

It is not brilliance, it is not ardour, and it is not loftiness that gives me of you that I adore you, with the light that goes away; it is gold, gold, it is the gold made shadow: your colour.

The colour of your soul; for your eyes are becoming it, and as the sun changes its golds for its reds and you become pale and melted, the gold made you emerge from your two eyes, which are my peace, my faith, my sun: my life! (The Landscape of the Soul, Juan Ramón Jiménez).

I love you, Allegria. I love you so much! I love your soul and everything it generates towards my life, good and only good".

Costantino (November 17, 1990)

This is how Costantino embarks on his journey to Germany to overcome the shadow and be free to love Allegria without restraint. What a desire, trying to defeat the shadow! It was humanly impossible what he desired. He lacked the strength to face the shadow. Only God can truly help you with a problem like that.

Chapter 5
**"There is no greater sorrow than to recall happiness in times
of misery".
Dante Alighieri**

Every human being is born with glory, like a star. We all have the talent to shine. We all have the glory of God included in our personalities. No one has ever come to this world without a touch of eternity. God put His light, sparkle, and deposit of creativity and ingenuity in every heart so every human can thrive.

Costantino had this heavenly deposit, but just as he had a talent for polishing and displaying it, he had a deep duality that prevented him from nurturing this dimension of his life.

On the one hand, his talent and his love for Allegria would allow him to shine at his best, but on the other hand, he felt love for the shadow, his passion for the darkness and the obscurity. That duality was lethal because it made him not whole at all.

In the kingdom of light, he was a "substitute"; in the kingdom of darkness, he recognised him as a "stranger, a weirdo" because there was still some light in him.

As the Bible puts it so clearly: "So, because you are lukewarm- neither hot nor cold- I am about to spit you out of my mouth" (Revelation 3:16), which would mean "but since you obey me only a little, I will reject you completely".

That was Costantino's problem. He wanted to be part of both kingdoms, on both sides, being loyal to both generals, the good and the bad, but in reality, he obeyed neither of them. He did not belong to any of the kingdoms.

In this world, you can't stand on the ledge. Either you're on one side or the other. It doesn't work when you take grey positions. Costantino was grey. That could be the colour that defined him. However, it couldn't be grey for long. It either turned white or took on black, but it couldn't be both.

The shadow is the sin. The sin that Costantino secretly cherished.

All sins are personal, producing an overall effect. Our conscience is designed to approve or disapprove highly. Costantino disapproved of what he was doing until that moment. He knew that what he was doing was wrong, knew it was his responsibility, and with what he was doing, he was hurting his family, his loved ones and Allegria.

When he gave up on himself to the shadow and felt qualms and guilt. He still had some fear of God, respect for God because he knew that God weighed all the attitudes and actions of the heart, that respect for God still preserved him in part as a member of the kingdom of light, but as he gave himself more and more to the shadow, his guilt evaporated, and his respect for God faded away, and he tried to rationalise or justify any sinful acts that he has committed.

The Holy Spirit guides us to the truth and makes us see our actions and true motivations. He still shows us the vanity or evil of our hearts. However, Costantino was silencing the voice of God. He wanted to mute it gradually. It was a tremendous internal battle being fought in Costantino's soul.

Satan, the prince of darkness, pushes him, threatens him, and even tortures his emotions so that he may fall more into the devil's kingdom. Maybe, that was what Costantino has become, a tortured soul.

***

Costantino was like King Saul, who ruled the people of Israel. King Saul had begun well. He had favoured before God and had tremendous support from the kingdom of light. Still, his duality slowly darkened him until the kingdom of light rejected him because he decided to embrace the kingdom of darkness because Saul always loved darkness more than light.

Saul was gorgeous, formidable and impetuous. The same prophet Samuel had described him as: "Here is the same man chosen by God to be your king! There's no one to compare him!". God had a group of brave men follow him, and Saul was one of them. The Spirit of God was upon Saul. God delivered him from all his enemies. All the people supported him. He was unstoppable. He was unique. He was God's chosen King.

Saul had two different essences, two opposing principles, two distinct characters and two unequal aspects in his person. The two forces couldn't coexist in the same space. Sooner or later, one would win, and the other would lose. That time he had come for Saul's life. Saul silently loved the shadow, his ego and his popularity. He loved all these over God's love.

Saul was beginning to rebel against God. The shadow had started to grow and rebel against God, which is as evil as resorting to mediums and fortune tellers. The prophet Samuel visited him and gave him his sentence: "It is not right to worship false gods or to disobey God. Since you want nothing to do with him, God wants nothing to do with you. God no longer wants you to be King because you did not want to do what He commanded. So I'm not going with you anymore."

Samuel would leave Saul forever. This means that the prophet of God would no longer accompany the King. Saul was alone in the darkness because he had decided that.

Samuel told him, "This is how God is going to take the kingdom of Israel from you, to give it to an Israelite better than you. The God who gives victory to Israel always keeps his word, does not change his mind, as people do".

Samuel left Saul forever, although he always felt great sadness for him. It also caused God to grieve as Saul's life decided to be lost. Saul loved darkness more than light. Ultimately, he loved the prince of darkness, his ego, his pleasures and even his popularity. He loved all these more than God and so was heart's Costantino.

If Allegria had known all this beforehand, she would not have undertaken this journey because it is not good to start without knowing the final destination. If she could have read the torment of his soul, in Costantino's eyes, she might have had the strength to escape the coming storm, but she had become blind with love. She was too naive to grasp the evil that Costantino hid in his soul. Allegria only saw the good in Costantino.

When Juliet met Romeo, she exclaimed, "Woe to me!". Perhaps this exact phrase would apply to the life of Allegria when she met Costantino, "Woe to me!" And by the time she gets to see the reality, she will say it with such regret, "Woe to me!".

***

At times, Costantino had times of peace, hours, and days when he wanted to become a man worthy of Allegria's heart. It was at that moment that his soul found calm. He thought of good things, Allegria's smile, enthusiasm, and vivacity. All those memories made him take paper and pencil to write letters to Allegria. That was Costantino's romantic and tender side. That side where he showed that he had noble feelings and even seemed to have a heart of gold, according to Allegria. This was one of his last moments when he had peace.

Costantino liked to read and write. He knew how to recognise who had the talent for writing too. He wrote one of his last letters to Allegria, always using the best poets such as Neruda, Borges and Alighieri.

Allegria:

"Don't go far off, not even for a day, because... because -- I don't know how to say it: a day is long and I will be waiting for you, as in an empty station

when the trains are parked off somewhere else, asleep.

Don't leave me, even for an hour, because then the little drops of anguish will all run together, and the smoke that roams looking for a home will drift

into me, choking my lost heart.

Oh, may your silhouette never dissolve on the beach; may your eyelids never flutter into the empty distance. Don't leave me for a second, my dearest, because in that moment you'll have gone so far I'll wander mazily over all the earth, asking, Will you come back? Will you leave me here, dying?" (Don't Go Far Off, Pablo Neruda).

Costantino (28 November 1990)

Reading this letter seems like a passionate declaration of love, but maybe it wasn't a declaration of love. Perhaps it was just a cry for help when he said that only in the hours he is visualising her are the moments when he has peace and, all worries disappear, the torment fades away.

Perhaps only when he thought of Allegria were the seconds when the torment did not come to strike his heart, which was already lost. Allegria did not understand all these signs of help, Allegria understood only love, so she confidently opened herself to it without suspicion.

In those last letters, too, there were omens of the outcome, where he expressed that he was not free to love.

Allegria:
"It is love. I will have to hide or flee. Its prison walls grow larger, as in a fearful dream. The alluring mask has changed, but as usual, it is the only one. What use now are my talismans, my touchstones: the practice of literature, vague learning, an apprenticeship to the language used by the flinty Northland to sing of its seas and its swords, the serenity of friendship, the galleries of the library, ordinary things, habits, the young love of my mother, the soldierly shadow cast by my dead ancestors, the timeless night, the flavour of sleep and dream?
Being with you or without you is how I measure my time.
Now the water jug shatters above the spring, now the man rises to the sound of birds, now those who look through the windows are indistinguishable, but the darkness has not brought peace.
It is love, I know it; the anxiety and relief at hearing your voice, the hope and the memory, the horror at living in succession.
It is love with its own mythology, its minor and pointless magic.
There is a street corner I do not dare to pass. Now the armies surround me, the rabble. (This room is unreal. She has not seen it)
A woman's name has me in thrall.
A woman's being afflicts my whole body". (The Threatened One, Jorge Luis Borges).
Costantino (December 2 1990)
This was Costantino's reality. Love came into his life, and he would have to decide whether he followed passion or followed it in the shade. It was a line he was supposed to draw. Either he'd stay on one side, or he'd move on.

"To be with you or not is the measure of my time". When he was with Allegria, it seemed he could see everything transparently and happily, but when he was far away from her, the shadow seemed to gather strength and fill everything.

The following sentence would define Costantino's torment well, "But the shadow does not leave me. The shadow has taken away my peace". When he was far from Allegria, the shadow covered everything, and the shadow and darkness visited him to transform him. Instead of being the excellent guy, Costantino, he became a monster.

For God's sake, he was a man fighting his demons. He was just a man trying to defeat his monsters! An impossible task for the human race. It's impossible. An individual can't beat hell. Never.

***

Allegria was Italian; as a good Italian, she had read Dante Alighieri. Costantino knew about Allegria's fascination with Dante, so, in the desperate act of gaining her acceptance and not losing her because he was far away, he wrote a fragment of The Divine Comedy, where he felt like Dante, idealizing his Beatrice, a being so angelic and full of light.

Allegria:

"La mia bocca abrá ardori di geenna. La mia bocca sará per te un inferno di dolcezza e seduzione. Gli angeli della mia bocca troneggeranno sul tuo cuore. I soldati della mia bocca ti prenderanno d'assalto. I preti della mia bocca incenseranno la tua belleza. La tua anima si agiterá como una regione durante il terremoto. I tuoi occhi saranno carichi allora di tutto l'amore che si é accumulato negli sguardi dell'unamnitá da quando esiste. La mia bocca sará un esercito contro di te un esercito pieno di contrasti. Vario como un incantatore che sa variare le sue metamorphosis. L'orchstra e i cori della mia bocca ti diranno il mio amore. Te lo sussurra di lontano. Metri gli occhi fissi sull'orologio attendo il minuto stabilito per l'assalto" *(Apollinaire, Dante Alighieri).*

Costantino (December 10, 1990)

Something strange about him; sometimes, Costantino felt guilty of conscience and remorse because he knew how dirty and tormented his soul was. He knew he was not free to love Allegria, but he still encouraged her more towards this love. Either he should have been brave enough to take all the steps forward to become fully involved in Allegria's life, or he should have disappeared entirely from her life without giving hope to Allegria's heart and making her fall in love.

This game was like a slow seduction to hell. To Costantino's hell. She wasn't smart enough to realise what it was about, so she could have run off to save her life.

It was like stepping onto the fire, not knowing it would hurt you, and hallucinating that you will have a better future when your life is slowly heading for the worst experience.

Allegria, as Dante did with his Beatrice, thought she could get him out of hell, but no human being could get another human being out of hell. Every human being needs to fight a personal battle. Every human needs to learn to be free with the help of heaven. It's a personal battle. Either heaven helps you, or you're alone. Heaven is on your side, or you'll break down sooner or later.

***

Time was passing, and Christmas was approaching. Costantino said he'd be back before Christmas.

Christmas was special for Allegria. She looked forward to the holidays because she knew she would meet Costantino.

The markets in Aosta were filled with a beautiful Christmas atmosphere. The whole city of Aosta was splendidly decorated for the celebration, lights, trees, Christmas carols, beautiful mangers with typical details, Santa Claus, nougats, sweet bread, turkeys, roast meat, everything was ready to receive Christmas. That's how the heart of the Alps was.

There was a programme of visits and tastings at the city's markets in preparation for the arrival of the festivities. Typical dinners at each house in anticipation of Christmas. All this was designed so that everyone could visit the beautiful Christmas markets of Aosta, a city that was full of charm in the heart of Saint-Vincent's historic centre; the visit included the famous "Marché Vert Noel", the Christmas market set in the incomparable setting of the Roman Theatre, in the centre of Aosta.

Christmas in Aosta that smelled of snow, first, hot wine and spices. Christmas in Valle d'Aosta has the candor of snow. Christmas in Valle d'Aosta tastes like a perfect Christmas. It has the warmth of stories and fire in a fireplace, games, and laughter between friends. Between November and January, the "Marché Vert Noel" Christmas market transforms a corner of the city, the Roman theatre, into an alpine village. There you could find exquisite local specialities, wines, handicrafts, yesteryear objects, Nordic inspirations, and small luxuries within everyone's reach to breathe together the air of celebration!

Every day, visitors could browse the streets of the village in search of a gift among the many handmade products: candles, soaps, ceramics, wooden objects, antique furniture, articles and accessories made of wool and felt, hemp, lace, Christmas decorations, typical Valdostan gastronomic products, sweets and pastries, objects created with the technique of découpage or other manual methods. All of Aosta was covered in snow. It was the perfect view. It was the perfect Christmas.

Allegria's favourite Christmas carol was "Joy to the world; the Lord has come". She wanted the world to be delighted, as happy as she and the whole city of Aosta were. Allegria's smile illuminated her entire atmosphere, as did all of Aosta's lights in that month.

***

Christmas week arrived, and Allegria received no letters, no news. The 24th came, and it was just silence. He didn't come. He didn't show up.

Can you imagine at that moment how Allegria felt?

To say she was devastated is an understatement.

All her make-up faded, her blue dress crumpled, and her smile turned to tears. He never came, he never arrived, and her blue dress wrinkled, and this love is no longer love. She went to sleep crying slowly. Her heart was hurt.

No. This was no longer her love. Costantino was no longer her love. Allegria got tired of the style of Costantino. He would come and go when he wanted; it was like an omen that this love had never been love.

Allegria would never know what happened regarding Costantino's secret, his love-hate relationship with the shadow. All this was a world apart that Allegria did not even imagine.

The poetries, the letters, the bicycle rides, the kisses, and the caresses were carried away by the wind, and when it was an actual date, in real-time and in the real world, Costantino was not there for Allegria. Costantino was never there. Allegria was alone; all she had were promises, poetry, affection and the romance of an absentee.

They say that the love of your life is not the one that makes your legs tremble but the one that brings balance to your life. Costantino, made Allegria's legs shake, but he was never there when he had to be there.

Allegria should have realised there that Costantino was not the love of her life. He did not produce balance and peace in her soul, but on the contrary, everything was torment and misery, profound pain that increased with time. Costantino loved the shadow more than he loved her. However, could so many love letters be wrong? Could so many poems and so many declarations of deep love be a mistake?

That was something Allegria could never understand.

***

What happened was that in Allegria's mind, sincerity and integrity always prevailed. She couldn't imagine that people could do one thing and say something completely different without really feeling it.

Costantino could still copy poems without really putting his soul into them. She has never thought people could be so mean as to play with somebody's feelings.

With all this happening, Allegria's family no longer accepted Costantino. The Disalvatore family began to keep an inevitable obfuscation towards Costantino because they saw in him a certain degree of falsehood, the lie of an illusion.

The Disalvatore family thought that Costantino did not love Allegria. They felt that this was not love, at least not true love. The Disalvatore family wouldn't accept Costantino and would tell Allegria to stop loving him because he wasn't worth it.

Allegria should have taken that advice. However, she was naive in this game of love. She believed that others did not understand the love that Costantino professed to her. How many pains would Allegria avoid if she had listened to that advice?

Nobody understood that weird love. In the end, one decides whether to love or not. One takes the initiative to continue increasing something or to finish it. Allegria should have stopped, stepped aside and closed her heart. She should have stopped loving him.

Sincerely she was getting tired of him, and from the bottom of her heart, she was already starting to freeze.

Maybe Allegria was asleep in the deception, and it was time to wake up. As Katy Perry's song "Yeah, I was in the dark, I was falling hard, with an open heart, I'm wide awake, How did I read the stars so wrong... And now it's clear to me that everything you see ain't always what it seems... Yeah, I was dreaming for so long; I wish I knew then what I know now… Wouldn't dive in, Wouldn't dive in, wouldn't bow down, gravity hurts, you made it so sweet, till I woke up on the concrete, falling from cloud nine, crashing from the high, I'm letting go tonight... Not losing any sleep, I picked up every piece and landed on my feet... I'm wide awake; yeah, I am born again".

It was time to let Costantino go completely. It was time to be free from him, of the idea of him, of his poems, of his absences, of his silences and even of his presences. It was time to embrace freedom once again.

The funny thing is that he was the one who was in the dark, but he made her feel like she was part of the darkness with the loneliness and torment that made her go through.

Costantino had a dark soul, and Allegria had a soul full of light, but he introduced her into the darkness of sadness, and her light was weakening, even though, at one point, her light was so intense before his arrival.

Chapter 6
"In the middle of the journey of our life, I came to myself
within a dark wood
where the straight way was lost".
Dante Alighieri

Allegria was devastated by the wickedness of Costantino. He was a pain all over her. She believed with such a pure heart in that love, but everything turned out to be false and deceitful. She should have left some room for doubts and questions about that love before believing it, but she hadn't thought that way.

How hard it must be to love a tortured person, how hard it must be to love a dark person disguised as light! Because you don't know if it's light or dark. All these thoughts went through Allegria's mind.

Costantino sensed he had made a mistake. One more mistake, his pool was full of errors; Allegria didn't want to swim more in his love's pool. Maybe he wanted to make up for his wrongdoing. Perhaps he was fighting to be part of the light. No one knows what motivated him, but he published a book inspired by his love story.

He went to a small publishing house, took his whole draft of poems and decided to publish his poems. His love for Allegria had inspired him to write sweet poems. Since he met Allegria, he dared to make all his writings public. Allegria inspired courage in him.

It took two months. The publisher was a small one, and as he had worked for years in a bookstore, he knew friends and had contacts based on the family he represented to know which publisher would have the resources and the will to publish his ideas. By February, the book had been released. It was titled "For Her". In the dedication, he wrote: "Because you make me brave."

Allegria was in Aosta, continuing her life as usual, and she had slowly forgotten about Costantino. He was practically no longer a part of her life, although sometimes it appeared in her thoughts. She decided to go into a bookstore to buy books and into the "new" sector, she saw the name of Costantino Habsburg. The book "For Her." Her whole world stopped. She was frightened, and her knees weakened. Allegria didn't know if what she would read would be good or bad. She feels that even her blood pressure has dropped.

She decided to take one book and go to the cash register. She'd buy one. She had to read it.

She came running home and opened it. She began to read it, poem after poem. Among the dozens of poems, they stood out before her eyes and touched her heart because they subtly seemed to be talking about her:

We were...
I can feel your breath.
Caressing my heart
Making it feel alive
And vibrating with every beat

Looking us straight into each other's eyes
And as I close them, I can feel your lips getting closer
Dying of nerves at this moment
Wanting everything to be perfect

Your lips are on mine.
And I'm closer to you.
Than I've ever been
And yet I can say
Nothing has been proven

It hasn't been proven.
Love was already there.
For as long as I've known you, it's been
But now I'm sure
That I never want to part from you.

Those first emotions of love they had felt again were beginning to awaken in Allegria's heart. That sweet love knocked again on the door of Allegria's soul.

I dreamt of you...
We were walking together by the sea.
The dream was perfect,
I didn't want to open my eyes; I didn't want to wake up.

I could have fallen asleep to death

And I know he would have died in peace
But I don't want to dream about you anymore.
I want our love to be a reality.

When you wake up
See you
And know that I can hug you.

And the poems continued to rekindle Allegria's heart.

It's you
You're the woman of my dreams
But not the woman of my reality.
Because my reality is dark, sad and cold
And I know I can't hug you.

Although I confess that sometimes,
I daydream; I dream that I am with you
and I can hug you.

I want to live with you forever, by the sea.
Life was perfect there, God, you and me;
No darkness.

But the darkness has already become part of me,
The night takes me away from your smile and wraps me
mercilessly.
When I remember your smile, my soul is filled with peace.

I know that tonight, when I close my eyes,
For a moment, I will leave the darkness
And my soul will come running to you,
and even if it is just a dream,
Just a plan, I will embrace you again; my light, my peace.

In that poem, Costantino better than ever described his reality.

That's who you are
Tender like no one else

Innocent, just like you
Almost to the point of becoming naive

I will never hear you,
Any offensive words
You only claim if you feel I'm walking away.

Well, you value friendship
love and forgiveness.

Words of encouragement
It's what comes out of your mouth.
A Guiding Look
And you never hurt me
because you lead me to mercy.

A love that is born inside you
You don't say anything more, but I may feel
And know that you'll be there for me
That you will never let me go.
Someone I can always count on...
You, the flame of life, gladden my walk in this darkness.

What a statement Costantino made. It seemed to be Allegria's pure goodness, but sometimes love can not only be good, sometimes it must also be firm. That was something Allegria had to learn.

***

How incredible is fate
To end up here with you
Always love each other so much
Falling in love like when I first saw you.

I fell in love
But you know what? I wasn't expecting this.
To be by your side
I am constantly feeling full and relieved.

And what more could I ask for
If with you I have everything
Seeing the world with different eyesight
Eyes that light up my darkness.

Such darkness; how I wish I could be free to love you!

Allegria's tears rolled down as she was reading poem after poem, and then began the worst part, the omen that the darkness was overcoming Costantino and that all this love was going to end, for that was what the book declared.

I wish I could break free to love you
Shadow, please don't make me leave her!
I couldn't live without her.
Without her voice, without her peace.

I know you think she isn't good for me,
That she isn't the ideal one,
That light and darkness are not compatible.

Shadow, I know you are weak in the light and the truth.
Shadow, you look at her; you long to be near her.

But the light beats you,
And she defeats you just by passing by.
Shadow, you devour my feelings; you hide my truth.

But I won't blame you... it would be unfair
Well, that woman is perfect.
And she may defeat the darkness without mercy.

And how could I know... if I love her just the same?
If only when I just saw her
She filled my caves with light as no other had done before.
And I get lost in her smile
Without thinking about anything else.

And that's how I stayed as a child,

Admiring her wisdom
And listening to her talk.
And even if I look like a fool
I don't care about what people may say.

Well, I'd do anything for her,
Anything to stay close to her.
That doesn't count, though,
Because I know that the shadow defeats me every day.
No twists and turns; that's my reality.

Sometimes I think I have no escape from the shadow of her,
Because I'm weak inside,
I'm weak, and I wouldn't say I like the kindness she irradiates,
Not before so much evil of my heart, my darkness.

And so I hope it remains.
The secret in my mind,
Well, if she ever finds out
Maybe she could collapse.

And I prefer to suffer and love her in silence
To lose her in my attempt to confess my reality.
Well, to lose her completely
I would die forever in my darkness.
My damned darkness!

As she reads the poem, Allegria can't stand it any longer and bursts into tears. She was already realizing that they had lost.

We have lost
A moment that has never been,
Words I have never uttered,
A hug I have never given,
Tears that have never shed.

Fire of the heart that did not ignite,
The warmth of the soul that has not sheltered me,
And the "I love you too."

That has never been uttered.

It was just a dream,
A deception of the heart,
A trap that, in the end,
Made me die from love.

Allegria knew when she read that poem that there was no hope and that the love between them had wholly perished.

When there was hope
I was terrified of the words
That may come from your mouth,
I had been waiting for the right time,
And it went through without realizing it.

I didn't expect it that way,
Then I lost you.
It couldn't have gone any worse,
And I failed to tell you my feelings.

I guessed what you'd say,
With a hug, the farewell was sealed.
I didn't want to let you go... I liked the moment to be eternal.
That moment could be everlasting.

And even though the hug is over,
I think maybe I do deserve all this,
Because deep down, I think I loved
More darkness than light.

That was the truth of Costantino's heart, and Allegria had to know it; Costantino was charmed with darkness more than light.

***

How hard it is to keep thinking
About something that no longer exists.
How hard it is to keep talking

About us while you have already gone.

How can I stop crying,
If it is impossible to get a smile on my face?
How to stop loving you so much,
If I don't want to let you go yet?

And I don't know if I'm going to make it,
How could I stop my love for you from growing?

How to understand
That your love for me is going to end?
And there's nothing to be done,
All I can do is wait.

How hard it is to keep loving you
Since you're only in my mind.
And how hard it is to explain the time,
I can't wait for you any more.

That poem was like a farewell letter; at that moment, Allegria couldn't stand it any longer and began to cry without consolation because it is one thing to imagine that you are losing someone important in your life and another thing to know that you have already lost him.

Allegria knew that time had buried them and that they had to go their separate ways without waiting any longer.

 As the Latin musician Samo would sing: "Tienes que soltar mi mano y seguir tu camino, tienes que apagar tu llanto y decirme adiós, sé que yo perdí tu amor en un simple descuido, cuando pude abrir los ojos, ya no éramos lo mismo.

Se apagaron las estrellas que tú y yo encendimos, dentro tuyo se hizo piedra todo ese dolor, tuve el cielo entre tus brazos y lo eche al vacío, por creer que estaba escrito en las hojas del destino.

Doy un paso atrás, vete ya no intentes regresar, vete ya no intentes regresar, es hora de borrarme de tus labios, porque ya no quiero hacerte daño, tienes que escapar ya no te detengas a mirar, este corazón lleno de espinas que te lastima, doy un paso atrás.

Tienes que encontrar tu sueño lejos de mi vida, y guardar en el olvido el eco de mi voz, por qué no aprendí a escuchar cuando tenías frío, por creer que estaba escrito en las hojas del destino.

Doy un paso atrás, vete ya no intentes regresar, es hora de borrarme de tus labios, porque ya no quiero hacerte daño, tienes que escapar ya no te detengas a mirar… tienes que soltar mi mano y seguir tu camino".

English translation:

"You have to let go of my hand and go your way; you have to turn off your tears and say goodbye to me; I know that I lost your love in a simple carelessness; when I could open my eyes, we were no longer the same.

The stars that you and I lit were extinguished, and inside you, all that pain turned to stone; I had the sky between your arms and threw it away for believing it was written on the pages of destiny.

I take a step back, go away and don't try to come back, go away and don't try to come back; it's time to erase me from your lips because I don't want to hurt you anymore, you have to escape and don't stop to look at this heart full of thorns that hurts you, I take a step back.

You have to find your dream far from my life and keep in oblivion the echo of my voice; why didn't I learn to listen when you were cold, for believing that it was written in the leaves of destiny?

I step back, go away, no longer try to come back; it's time to erase me from your lips because I don't want to hurt you anymore; you have to escape, no longer stop to look... you have to let go of my hand and go your way".

That's what she was determined to do; Allegria had to let Costantino's hand go and move on. Costantino had become a total stranger to Allegria; in her mind, she was determined to forget him, although her heart told her otherwise.

I am aware that I don't know what I'm living for,
But I'm willing to learn.
I don't know if I would be a good student,
But no better teacher I could have chosen.

And I can't deny I'm not afraid,
That I'm not scared of my ignorance.

I've put all my trust in her.
And that she won't ever hurt me, I remain hopeful.

And there's nothing else left but that,
But I know it's worth the risk.
And if this ends, even though I don't want to,
I know it will always be the most beautiful memory I've ever had.

That was the last poem. They talked about themselves and their wishes but could not be together because the darkness inside him was more substantial than all the light she could radiate.

Allegria struggled with loving or not loving him, whether she should leave him in oblivion forever or be a guardian angel to help him save himself.

However, we are all well aware of the saying, "Who risks being a saviour dies on the cross". Allegria, on the one hand, wanted to risk her life to save him, even though this would condemn her to her crucifixion because crucifixion would come, as everything in life comes: age, accounts, responsibilities, duties, bills, but on the other hand, she already wanted to take the step back and forget about him forever.

Loving him would be like enjoying a little story at first, but with a catastrophic ending that no one would want to experiment with.

Poor Allegria, she should have run away from him, from his shadow and let it all end in peace; she should have taken the step back when she was determined to take it!

Nevertheless, there she was, ready to give her life so the coming tragedy would not happen. It's like standing before the train, dreaming that it will stop or wanting to stop a plane with your hand, preventing time from passing, the shadow from growing, and everything from being like before. Something impossible, absolutely impossible.

Battling through the dilemma of whether to continue this story, the doorbell of her home rang one morning when the sun was shining brighter than ever. She came out to open the door, and there he was, Costantino.

Seeing her with those beautiful blue eyes, it was as if all the doubt had disappeared, she smiled, and she hugged him; he sighed in relief, and it was like everything was starting all over again.

Chapter 7
"No one thinks of how much blood it costs."
Dante Alighieri

Costantino invited Allegria for a tour of Courmayeur, an autonomous region of Valle d'Aosta. Courmayeur has a beautiful view of the Alps, picturesque landscapes, and gorgeous mountain scenery. This Italian city is a tourist attraction. This destination has become one of Europe's most popular ski destinations in winter.

Courmayeur is also chosen as a summer tourist destination for simple relaxation and its natural attractions, such as the Veny Valley or the Ferret Valley. Mountain climbers and hikers are, therefore, often present in summer.

Courmayeur is the site of the famous Tour of Monte Bianco (Mont Blanc), which surrounds the entire massif in several stages, passing through France, Italy and Switzerland.

When Costantino and Allegria decided to go out, that day was a beautiful spring day in May, winter had passed, and everything was blooming.

In Courmayeur were the handicraft fairs where they showcased everything the artisans produced with wood from the Alps, metal, Valdostane stones, decorative items, and so many other things made in the area. This is the reason why the place becomes crowded during May.

In Courmayeur, you can walk around the different squares and have gelato with unique flavours like Bacio and Monte Bianco. It's just a fantastic experience.

That was a splendid day, and Allegria asked permission at work to enjoy this day with Costantino. Courmayeur was enlightened. On that day, everything seemed happy.

Costantino and Allegria went for a walk. They looked at each other and laughed; they hardly spoke, though. They repeatedly whispered, "Honey, I've missed you"; "Sweetie, I've missed you so much".

Costantino told her how much he had missed her and never stopped thinking about her. She hugged him and said she had missed him so much and couldn't understand how he could have disappeared for all those months.

He tried to make it up for his mistakes, explaining that she never left his mind but that he needed to overcome things. He needed to put his whole world full of shadows in the past.

She asks him if he has managed to put his life in order, to reduce the shadows, but he replies: "I couldn't, maybe they have even grown up, maybe I think I can never overcome them, they are very strong, very intense. One day I'm fine, then relapse after two or three days. I tell myself that I'll get over it and be fine. Still, the shadow gets me back again". Allegria sighs and says sadly, "Costantino, I think you're tormented. Maybe I can never help you. It is difficult to have a relationship with someone like you". Costantino takes her hands firmly and exclaims, "Please do not leave me. If you leave me alone, I will run to the shadows, and believe me. It will be hell for me. You are the hope of heaven that I harbour with deep hope".

At that point, Allegria should have been strong enough to say, "I don't think I can; I can't give my life to you. I'm worth it, I also matter, and I can't have a relationship with someone as toxic as you, someone who one day is fine and then has two or three hellish days".

However, she hasn't; perhaps she thought she could do the work of a saviour and become the gate for him out of that hell.

***

The problem is that nobody can get you out of hell, absolutely nobody. Only God can get you out of there. Your will can help, too, because you will have to fight against what is pushing you down. No one can fight your battles. Your battles and victories are personal. No one can fight in your place. You have to conquer and solve your problems with God's help.

Costantino tries his best to keep her cheerful so she would give up the idea of abandoning him. He invites her that night to dinner at his parent's house, where his brothers, uncles, and cousins, all of whom would be gathered to celebrate Costantino's return to the city.

She kindly agreed; however, the happiness was not complete; it's like when you receive something you expected, but it turns out that what you received caused you sadness and disappointment because it wasn't as fabulous as you imagined.

Well, that's how Allegria felt. She was receiving something beautiful, a formal invitation to the Habsburg house. What else could she ask for? At the same time, that invitation was full of shadows, sadness and bad omens. It's just like something you desire so badly, but in the deepest side of your heart, it makes you sad, and you start to reject what they're giving you. Allegria would have the chance to be with the Hapsburgs and to be Costantino's official girlfriend.

At times Allegria was deluded and decided to love Costantino. That love was like walking on thorns. All circumstances would hurt her. She was trying to mitigate the pain, keeping her mind focused, only seeing the bliss at the end. However, there will not be a happy ending.

Costantino would make her go through hell because he lived in hell himself. You can only give what you have!

At that moment, Allegria should have "spread her wings, reached for the clouds and kissed them", as the group Maná will sing in the song "Tengo muchas alas". The sun was smiling, allowing her to escape Costantino's infernal claws. She should have run out to catch the sun, not to stay tied to Costantino since Allegria had many skies to fly. There was a lot of wind for her to lift her wings and fly. However, she decided to see the sun from afar, staying beside Costantino.

Allegria wants to look her best at the dinner. She got ready for that night as if it was the big night. She wore her best blue dress of the nineties, which looked fantastic on her white complexion. She gently put on some makeup and was ready for dinner.

Costantino picked her up and told her she looked terrific; he even started singing Eric Clapton's song 'Wonderful Tonight' while driving her to his place.

When she arrived, the first one to greet and be kind to her was Costantino's father. Oh yes, the Duke of the Business had the grace and kindness to be attentive to a commoner. Maybe at that moment, Allegria imagined her story would be like Cinderella's. No wonder how naive Allegria was!

The mother was also generally friendly, although she had an air of Duchess that made her difficult to deal with. His siblings were polite. At least, that's what they looked like.

Dinnertime comes, and everyone starts talking about politics, crises, finances, the church, the world, how amazing Steffi Graf was, the terror of drug trafficking in Colombia with Pablo Escobar, Germany wanted to be reunited, that democracy had returned in Chile, Fujimori was the president of Peru, the war in the Gulf had broken out, Yugoslavia had split apart, the war in Bosnia, USSR will finally be defeated soon, and that the business was to open more video clubs.

Yes, it was the '90s. Those were the kind of conversations at a family dinner. It was a very informative dinner. The good news is that Allegria was not uninformed and could follow the thread of the whole conversation.

There was so much to discuss but nothing to talk about it. They were talking about news and information, not hearts. No personal questions. They skipped private conversations such as: "Hello, Allegria, how have you been? What do you do for a living?" Nothing. Perhaps it was because, deep down, the mother understood the duality of her son, and she did not intend to struggle with a young lady who was there just that day and might be gone the next day.

***

Sometimes, when you set a goal, it is then when the enemies appear. If Allegria wanted something for her life, thousands of enemies would appear.

Poor Allegria! It wasn't just the family. It was the society in which Costantino lived, the whole community itself, where the prostitutes were the stars, the brainless were the ones who moved the masses, and the ungodly were the ones who were promoted. Do you know how frustrating it is to be excellent in a mediocre society? Costantino loved that world, that society and even the system.

Allegria disagreed with that system. She did not give in to that system. There is a saying, "The world loves you if you belong to it". That world loved Costantino and his family because they belonged to the world. They were part of that whole world. Costantino's family represented part of that system.

Allegria rejected the system of promoting the worst ones while leaving aside the best ones, praising mediocrity and ignoring excellence, that system of controlling hearts and people instead of learning to control yourself.

Allegria didn't belong there. She should have noticed that at that dinner. Allegria did not belong to that world. That world that loved Costantino but turned Allegria into an outcast.

It wasn't just Costantino's family. It was society itself.

Do you know how horrible it is to live in a society where everyone has a price? Where the most airheaded man is the one who handles the baton, where the most influential prostitute is praised for promoting all kinds of evil or where being a prostitute is the way to reach your achievements, to get to the top.

In a society where the evil one will have a voice. Just imagine how sick a society can be where imbecility, prostitution, and evil have constant representatives.

There was no place for dignity, honour, virtue and purity. That society was hell. It was like hell itself. You know what it means to live in a community where everything is like this and only like this, without solid voices in favour of good, other examples, and different horizons of better conditions.

Poor Allegria, she'd better flee for her life! Allegria should have opened her eyes and understood what kind of society she didn't want to be a part of. Still, no, at that moment, she idealised everything, even what society meant to her. She believed that she could improve everything, even if that society may harm goodness. What a delusion!

The system was rotten, and when the system is terrible, there's no point in fighting for a change; you'd better run for your life and find a better plan. No one can change a corrupt, rotten, toxic system. No one becomes genius and virtuous overnight; society does not light up overnight. If a system only values prostitution and stupidity, that society will take three generations to learn to think differently.

Each generation spans forty years. It will take one hundred and twenty years to think differently.

In short, Allegria still did not understand the evil and filthiness she was facing. She believed that she could change everything for the better. What she did not realise was that she would fight against hell itself.

So Allegria was trying to please this society, to be accepted in a world that alienates her. While in reality, in this life, one does not have to try to be accepted. One is accepted or not. Period. One does not have to strive to be understood, loved, valued, or respected by others. The person who will love you will accept you as you are, with your strengths and weaknesses. That's true love, accepting the whole package.

However, Allegria was trying to smile and be accepted by everyone, by Costantino, by society, by the system, by a damn system that didn't even deserve her effort.

Why do people love to get involved in impossible causes? At that point, Allegria had the strength to fight for the cause. However her strength would not last long, and she would become weaker day by day. That was another truth she was unaware of at that time.

***

Remember the movie Shrek? He's an ogre living in a swamp, a filthy place, no place for fantasy and hope. The swamp is invaded by characters sent by the "evil Lord Farquaad". Many things happen in history, but the main thing is that Shrek meets a princess, they fall in love, and instead of him becoming a prince and improving himself, she gets worse, bringing out the worst in her, making her look like an ogre forever.

Why doesn't he become an actual prince? Why doesn't Shrek chance for better? Why does she have to get worse? Kind of like today's society. There are some men of low quality; then the woman degrades herself, leaving her position of lady, only to promote the wild instincts in him.

We also see that there are men who have good quality, who are gentlemen but are seduced by women of low quality, and then they degrade themselves, leaving their place as gentlemen to be after whores.

Today we have the scourge of Shrek, women who degrade themselves to settle down with a man who is not a prince but an ogre! A filthy ogre. Or we have men who degrade themselves to be with whores, leaving their gentleman's seat.

Love elevates, not degrades.

A famous phrase says, "In a world full of Kardashians, be Marie Curie, be a lady". Be virtuous and decent, be a lady in your way of being and leading, a woman of values who contributes to a better community with her talents and abilities. Be a productive and dignified woman for society.

Of course, the same applies to men; let them be the Galileo Galilei of their generation. Men who contribute with their talents and conduct to build a better society.

Fiona turned into something worse, not something better. She changed herself to be with the ogre. When we have a life full of sins and filthiness, we become "ogres".

In Cinderella's story, she is an excellent young lady who serves and helps others. Therefore she becomes a princess because doing and giving goodness will always bring good outcomes.

Goodness is a superpower; you will reap all the good you sow.

Cinderella is good for that reason; she finds a good man who turns out to be an actual prince in her path.

In the story of Shrek and Fiona, both become the worst version of themselves. This is how we can describe the performance of Costantino and Allegria. Allegria was a princess. She was not under any spell. She was a beautiful and dignified woman for society, productive and intelligent, he was an ogre, and by introducing her into his world, he brought out the worst in her because he ruined her as a person.

He woke her up to a cruel, dirty, filthy world. Costantino was slowly turning Allegria into someone to live with him as an ogre. Of course, the whole system worked together to bring out the worst in her because that world didn't motivate her to be a lady because only prostitutes seemed to reign in that world.

What an ugly thing to live in a system where prostitutes are queens and buffoons are the powerful voices, poor Allegria. Run for your life as soon as you can! Your life is worth much more than all that!

Everyone chooses what they want. That was the moment for Allegria to choose well, to save herself, but no, she had decided to be part of Costantino's life. She had agreed to enter hell.

***

Everyone chooses which one to love and serve. Costantino had chosen the shadow, and Allegria had chosen Costantino. Can you imagine how all that could end? Yes, in hell!

Idolatry prevents you from seeing other options. Idolatry prevents you from seeing God and all of God's beautiful answers for your life. That was Allegria's problem; she idolised Costantino, and idolatry is a grave sin in front of God because it makes one content with inferior glory.

Idolatry deforms the heart because it causes us to be content with something far inferior to what God desires to give us and to take a minimal form for ourselves by making us become the image that our idol assigns us when in reality, we can have the idea that God Himself desires to give us, which is excellent and full of splendour. The glory of God makes us develop all our dimensions. However, human idolatry drives us to take a small and not proper form of ourselves. It is an insult to God to reject the glory He wants for us and to accept the glory humans want to give us. When we idealise or idolise someone, we get a credit utterly inferior to the one we were designed for.

Tell me who you idolise, and I'll let you know what you become.

That is the problem with our society. It idolises people and therefore distorts order and truth. Prostitutes, bandits, singers, actors, mobsters and many others are idolised but are just flesh and blood. Instead of reflecting the Creator in all His strength, when we follow these idols, we become deformed as people accepting the cheap version of ourselves.

God created us to reflect His glory, character and splendour, not to yield to a deformity of ourselves.

The same thing happened with the people of Israel in the Bible. When Israel idolised people, false gods, money and positions, the society began to corrupt and deform itself.

Idols occupied the high places of the people and influenced and manipulated the community. They twisted it. Doesn't that sound like today? We see evil women at the top, the ungodly men running the society, and so the deformity of humanity is up in the air.

Why? Because a deformation system has been installed that does not honour God. Evil penetrated all sectors so much that a righteous and holy person finds himself struggling alone in the face of a degraded system that has been established.

"Blessed is the nation whose God is Lord" (Psalm 33.12). Idolatry deforms a society, but worshipping the true God, full of splendour and glory, makes the community rise. God raises individuals to develop their true gems. We were not born for so little. We were not born to reflect the glory of others. We were born to reflect His glory in our lives.

Idolatry is like accepting the wrong halo. Accept the "halo" of a human when you can have the halo of God himself.

Beyonce describes what it means to absorb someone's "halo" when she sings: "Everywhere I'm looking now, I'm surrounded by your embrace, Baby, I can see your halo, You know you're my saving grace, You're everything I need and more, It's written all over your face, Baby, I can feel your halo, Pray it won't fade away, I can feel your halo, halo, halo, I can see your halo, halo, halo".

She is accepting the halo of a man, the glory of a human.

Accepting human glory makes us deviate from the recognition that God wants to give us. Human glory makes us break the rules of good and wakes us up on an evil path.

Whenever we break God's established rules, we only get pain, anguish, depression and death because that alone produces sin: despair, suffering and death.

***

Allegria became dependent on the glory a man could give her instead of depending on the treasure God Himself could give her. She thought that Costantino was her hero, her saviour, a man of flesh and blood, who was limited, toxic, weak, evil and just a simple man.

She did too much for human glory until she broke the rules and hurt herself. Poor Allegria, she had to wake up, she had to wake up!

She thought she was entering the heaven of joy, love and tenderness, but in reality, she was entering the hell of pain, anguish and depravity.

Allegria should have needed to pray to lose Costantino's halo.

When a man truly loves a woman, he does not harm her, tries not to hurt her, and becomes a tremendous influence, someone who seeks goodness for her and has a protective effect. Costantino was the opposite of that. He was a halo of destruction.

Allegria needed to understand that she must never adore anyone except God. Please don't put a human being on a pedestal from which you think he will never fall because he will fail.

It's easy to admire Michelangelo's sculpture from afar, but when you get close, you start to see all the little cracks, and that was Costantino, a man full of horrible trials, which of course, from afar apparently were not seen.

***

The dinner was over, it was time to say goodbye, so Allegria greeted Costantino's family. At that time, the nicest one was Mr Habsburg, perhaps hoping that his son would get better and find a better path next to Allegria's smile. At the time, maybe there was hope.

They both leave Costantino's house, and he drives her home. He kisses her goodbye with a tender kiss, she goes to sleep, and duality begins to manifest itself in Costantino's life again.

That night Costantino couldn't sleep because he was thinking about the shadow.

***

Allegria and Costantino had agreed to go to the theatre together the next day. The Splendor Theatre was located on Via P. Pretoria, where they would see the play "Vacanze Romane", the most romantic musical comedy ever.

People worldwide have dreamed of this beautiful love story for over half a century, a timeless tale like Rome.

In this work, we see a man with Roman style in all his character, opposed by the ethereal elegance of Princess Anna, who is the force of pure feeling. The unforgettable Vespa ride in the shadow of the Colosseum continues to gather enthusiasm and recognition, arousing emotions and bringing the charm of Rome into the hearts of spectators from all latitudes.

Beautiful play they were predisposed to see. Of course, it would be attractive to see it with Costantino if duality did not exist in his life.

The next day they met, Allegria wore a beautiful dress inspired by the 1950s to accompany Costantino, in keeping with the event. He was waiting for her inside the car. He had a beautiful FIAT of the year and didn't even get off to greet her. He was like an ice floe.

It was the worst car trip Allegria ever had. The once warm, tender and in love, Costantino has turned out to be cold, distant and tortured. He expressed all his doubts with his attitude and gestures, making her feel completely uncomfortable.

Do you know how hard it is to be with someone who wants something one day and nothing the next? This duality in Costantino was sickly. At times, he found peace and tranquillity with Allegria, then the demons appeared to attack him, and his personality changed to the point where the demons possessed him, and hell broke loose.

It was like the demons were handling his personality. It just didn't seem like himself. Costantino was like King Saul of the Bible. Costantino had everything to be a brand-new king but didn't want to.

"How long will you mourn for Saul, seeing I have rejected him as king over Israel?" (1 Samuel 16.1). It is as if heaven were speaking to Allegria, "When are you going to wake up? He is not an honest person. He is a dual one".

It is as if the very spirit of God had abandoned Costantino, and an evil spirit had begun to torment him.

Allegria has become the best company that could be for Costantino. She was a young woman who pushed him towards goodness. She was brave and full of the spirit of God. She knew how to speak very well, a saint, wise, sensible, a woman who could inspire him towards goodness. However, Costantino was not interested in excellence. He preferred the other way around.

For moments when Costantino saw Allegria, he seemed driven towards grace and heaven. At times he caressed the idea of light and goodness, to abandon once and for all his dense darkness, but at times the spirit of evil manifested itself in Costantino, and everything became hell again.

***

Allegria accompanied Costantino in different church activities, hanging out and working. At times she was with him and helped him. In those moments, Costantino was so happy with Allegria that he could only think that he loved her.

Everything was going reasonably happily, as long as the demons didn't attack Costantino.

The Goliath would be fully revealed soon. The day came when the nightmare would fully reveal itself in front of Allegria.

It was an ordinary afternoon when Allegria took her bike and decided to go to Costantino's house for a snack. She was wearing one of those typical '90s headbands, bag-type shorts, and a flowery shirt, just like the boom of the moment.

She rang the doorbell and was received by Mrs Antonia, who worked at Costantino's house and kept the whole place in order. She indicated that Costantino was in his room, so she rushed upstairs, knocked on Costantino's door and waited.

Costantino tried to stop what he was doing, but she insisted. He hurried up, trying to hide what he had started. She knocked on the door again. When no one answers, she opens the door and finds the worst scene that she could find, the complete manifestation of the flesh, all the demons of Costantino in total exposure.

Costantino loved the shadow.

What she had just seen was so nasty that it may not be possible to describe in words. It was supernatural.

It is true that each person struggles with a few sins but struggles not to give in to them.

Whatever the name of the shadows or sins you are fighting with, you must know that all people who practice these shadows or sins cannot inherit heaven. Everyone faces temptations, and we all go through weaknesses. Still, with God's help, we can decide not to fall into that evil.

Every human eventually will have to decide "his sin or his Saviour, his sin or Jesus".

That afternoon, Goliath came out fully manifested, with his fury, strength and infernal splendour. That was when Allegria opened her eyes and saw the kind of hell she was involved in.

Costantino tried to caress her face to indicate that she saw nothing. However, for Allegria's soul, Costantino became a disfigured man. She stopped to see Costantino like a prince and began to see him like a great demon of the infernal legions, full of pus, claws, blood and a stinking smell, trying to caress her soul. She felt disgusted. She felt repulsion. She felt nauseous and cursed her fate at that moment, cursed the horrible day when Costantino crossed her path because she thought that she belonged to heaven, a place of light and glory, and did not deserve such a hideous fate. She could not associate herself with someone who was only part of hell but looked like a heavenly facade.

***

That was the right and exact moment for Allegria to leave, leave everything and never come back. However, she thought she might be the David that was needed at that time. She decided she could be brave, strong enough to beat Goliath.

Oh, Allegria, how deluded you are! No one can overcome another person's Goliaths. If that person does not rise and overcome his shadows, no one else can overcome those shadows for him.

Goliath presented himself with all his strength. He had all the heavy armour, necessary wealth, resources, and allies. As Allegria saw it, Goliath had all the power. Of course, we know that only God has all the true strength, and the heavens rule over the earth, but at that moment, in the eyes of Allegria, she was devastated and believed that all the power was gone.

Goliath had all the power, everything belonged to him because even had won the battle, and Allegria had nothing left; she was alone and even felt that she had been defeated.

When Allegria saw the disgusting figure of Goliath, it was as if she had been moved to hell. The whole environment changed. **She and Costantino were in the depths of hell.** They breathed dense darkness. They could not walk. All that surrounded them was thick darkness. They could not even see their hands, the smell was disgusting, and screams of horror were heard everywhere. They were in the depths of hell, at least that's what Allegria thought, but she hadn't seen the worst thing yet.

Goliath looked like a monstrous figure. He was enormous, with horns and rotten holes filling his body, and he had a spear. He drank blood. He had no mercy. Only hatred dwelled in him.

Hate, debauchery and evil were all that Goliath exhaled. It was ghastly. Allegria was shaking with fear. Goliath wore armour and looked invincible. He was invincible. Fire dragons accompanied him. He was not alone. He had a whole army behind him, thousands, millions of them. Allegria was the only one with white garments in that place because when they went down to hell, Costantino had been transformed; his white clothes now looked like rags and worse, he seemed to be one of them.

Costantino was already in favour of the enemy army, and Allegria was left alone. It would be nice to say that Allegria turned into David and beat Goliath in the middle of hell, but no, she couldn't. It was impossible because it wasn't her battle.

Costantino should have become David and defeated his Goliath, but he lacked that courage. Costantino was weak, foolish and dull because he did not know how to differentiate between the value of the passing and the eternal. He was enraptured with the passing pleasure, even though it would cost him eternity.

At that time, Allegria was living the reality of hell. Allegria saw, as in a vision, how living here on earth affected their eternity and saw some on their way to hell. The sad thing is that Costantino was there.

Allegria thought that Costantino would write his name in heaven for a glorious eternity, but no, Costantino was changing all his glory for scum and pain. One has to be stupid to do that!

That's human stupidity. Changes everything for the better to the worse. Goliath began to rant and curse God and all His creation, the hatred and evil that emanated were terrifying.

Fear overwhelmed Allegria, who was paralysed at the time.

Goliath insulted and said, "No one can ever defeat me, I am stronger than all of you, I am stronger than God Himself, the damned Jehovah, the damned God of Christians, I am the strongest, the greatest of all and among all!".

The hellish army cheered and cried out affirming this speech, praised him with raised hands, considered him their God and followed him to hell itself.

***

No one can stand against Jehovah. We know that Jehovah is the greatest and most powerful, but sometimes after hearing a lie so much, one may believe it. Allegria listened to that lie and sometimes doubted that Jehovah could defeat that legion. Goliath was not the devil himself, but he seemed.

If a Goliath produced such fear and chills, can you imagine what it would be like to face the devil himself? No one can. Only Christ has faced him and defeated him. However, Allegria was terrified and forgot everything she had learned in the Sunday church classes.

She knew inside her conscience and in the depths of her heart that Jehovah was and is the greatest, but before so much manifestation of hellish power, her flesh and her humanity began to fear and doubt.

Goliath had everyone enslaved. Everyone was chained to his orders, even Costantino. Goliath was the God of the flesh, unbridled pleasures and non-stop fetish. The charm itself, such as eating or sex, is not evil. It is wrong when such joy is done outside the law of God. Not because God is terrible but because doing something outside God's laws destroys you. Your sin does not harm God. Your sin harms yourself.

Goliath saw Allegria and began to insult her. Allegria was holy and pure. So you can imagine how Goliath starts to insult her. Allegria's purity was the target of all her mockery and offences because to belong to Goliath's army, a woman had to be promiscuous and sleep with many different men in her whole life, feeding the flesh of the men. Allegria saw how Goliath operated on the earth, providing Goliath's army for all these years.

All those kinds of women were in the cursed army. They were used as objects, compared, mistreated and bought as objects. They were paid for their services, and although this gave them an ounce of happiness for a moment, then came the actual bill; the bill of life "You will reap your sowing". Although they seemed to be very happy in this world, in reality, they were women tortured by hell because they attracted demons to themselves, and in the whole process, there was no love but lust.

They risked at any moment being discarded on Goliath's ladder because there were always others more beautiful or desired on the disgusting ladder to the summit. Then the ones above were discarded, and the next replaced the ones dislodged.

Could never be true love there. You could never find unconditional love there or be accepted for what your soul is worth. Never. However, even though these women looked so foolish pretending to enjoy that game, in reality, it was torture, they never had peace.

Heaven is the complete opposite of the system of hell. God treats you with dignity, honour, gentleness, modesty and unconditional love. However, they seemed to prefer to be treated like whores, because that is precisely what they were.

Life is a continuous path of choices, and at that moment, all the women were choosing that path. So Goliath pours all his hatred, contempt and evil into the purity of Allegria.

***

Allegria did not feel like David. She believed she could not fight Goliath. Why should she have to fight a battle that was not hers? After all, Goliat was not the giant that ruled over Allegria but the giant that Costantino faced.

At that moment, she thought it was time to get out of there, **"I have to get out of here"**, and she started running.

Allegria was wearing white and shimmering clothes. However, when she was running, she realised that the more she ran, the more she went into hell; she wasn't going up, she was going down.

Hell is a place of dense darkness, endless torment, and worse, without love and hope. Everything was under the dominion of the devil. All that was breathed was anguish, deep pain, and infinite affliction. The torture of the soul invaded everything. There was no peace, not a second of peace. The souls wanted to get out of there, but they could not.

It is as if Allegria could see a parallel world, souls who, by their actions, were preparing a place to dwell forever in hell for the endless torments. They were souls who were writing about their future in hell.

To serve evil does not pay well here on earth, much less for eternity.

Believe it or not, many souls made such a bad deal. There were souls sold to the devil who was in charge of that place. They sold their souls in exchange for fame, wealth and power. How can you love yourself so little to comfortably spend a few years here and eternity in straight horror?

The devil seduced the souls. The souls were serving him with complete devotion because they were under a delusion. The devil is the father of lies, so he made the souls believe that they were well and that the solution was coming, but when they realised the deception, the souls suffered the torment.

The devil gave them with one hand, but then he came to take them out with five hands. Everything that these souls achieved was in vain. Everything fell into a broken sack. They attained a minute of pleasure for then days and years of torment.

The devil made them believe they would achieve their goals, but these souls received nothing. It was all a constant hoax. Ruin always visited such souls because they had no true happiness, joy or peace. All they suffered was endless torments.

The souls worshipped the devil, but when the torment came, they cursed him. There was no peace. Just imagine the moment of the most incredible pain in your life. Now multiply that pain by countless times. Can you see the result? That's the result of the one who suffered the least in hell.

It was all gnashing of teeth, wailing from the depths of the heart and groaning for help. Everything was pain, anguish and desolation because God was not there, and it is impossible to have love when God is not there.

The demons, the legions, the principalities and the powers of darkness do not know what love is. They do not know how to have love, give love, mercy, pity, compassion, goodness and compassion.

All evil dwells in them, and as they live in such torment, they pierce the souls through that same torment. Can you imagine dwelling in such a hellish place? The worst thing is that foolish souls choose to embrace hell.

Since that was never God's intention, God did not create hell for human beings. However, all human beings have been endowed with free will and freedom of choice, and if they insist on rejecting

God, rejecting His ways and His goodness, there is nothing that can be done, the destiny is already set.

So much was the torment and anguish that Allegria experienced there that even though she did not belong there, she still felt the pain that others were suffering as if it were her own.

Allegria had to leave there but didn't want to go out alone. She had to find and get Costantino out of there because after they had gone to hell, Costantino's soul was lost among all the souls groaning with so much pain, so she didn't know where he was anymore.

***

Hell had four cardinal points as it was a territory like any other place. The east-to-west section was occupied by four principalities, winged, immense beings full of hatred and fire. They were giant monsters. The faces were utterly deformed.

They were the ugliest and most deformed of spiritual beings. There was nothing beautiful about them to admire. Terror personified them. They made you tremble with fear, and you could not escape their clutches; in fact, no one could get out of there alive. Their tongues were like snakes, like a mixture of animals and giants. Fingernails like claws. They all had a disgusting smell. Each of them had a name; one was called "Pride", the other "Greed", the third "Anger", and the fourth "Sloth".

The principality of "Pride" was so ruthless. It was arrogance personified, with the feeling of judgement towards others. Pride did not look suffering souls in the eye. Pride despised, bullied, intimidated, manipulated, used and discarded them, always mocking them. Pride hated them.

The principality of "Greed" had diamonds, gold and precious pearls all over its body. Still, when you approached it and looked at it clearly, everything turned to mud and mildew because nothing you can accumulate on this Earth has any real value in eternity.

"Greed" seemed beautiful, like a model in splendour, but on seeing it well, it was the most disgusting of all creatures, always self-conscious for not being more, for not being able to do more, for not achieving more, it was the ugliest principality of all, it was despicable.

The "Greed" wanted to boast of everything and obtain everything, but in reality, it got nothing. It was nothing. The souls under this principality were enslaved to achieve, be, and have more. It was constant torture. These souls could never be happy on earth. These poor souls did not realise that they were so deceived and were poor, blind and naked because God did not create us to have more, achieve more and be more than others. He created us to love and be loved, accept others and give and receive love.

Then there was the principality of "Anger". Fire and poison came out of his mouth; his only feeling was hatred. Whenever "Anger" opened his mouth, destructive fire consumed the souls below this principality. These souls, under the influence of the principality of Anger, hated everything; everyone hated each other. Hatred was the constant.

At the moment when the souls were consumed by the fire of "Anger", they groaned for help. When the fire went out for moments, these souls were left crashed, and everything started again. The souls came back to life, and the torment continued. Chains of hatred, resentment, quarrels, enmity, jealousy, strife, and contention bound these souls. They were souls with everything to be happy here on earth, but they lived from quarrel to quarrel, from conflict to conflict, from war to war. The fighting, the hatred, the Anger and the rage were constant in their lives. They lived in continual torment.

Then followed the principality of "Sloth". Everything looked so dirty in that section of hell, so disgusting, because "Sloth" loves dirt, laziness, and real abandonment.

Chaos was the constant. This would be like a minor principality, but no, quite the contrary. Because of Sloth, the principalities of "Anger", "Greed", and "Pride" became more vigorous.

When one does not do what one must, one loses responsibility, so evil advances.

Pride nurtures laziness, with typical excuses such as: "I'm not going to do that little work because I'm worth more than that", with the reason of belittling certain types of work fuelling laziness.

Pride not to clean, not to help, not to work, not to do. All of this brought more strength to the principality of Sloth, making it stronger and thus strengthening the principality of Pride at the same time. Laziness was, after all, arrogance personified.

Greed was based on Sloth because most people wanted to get more but without effort. While God blesses the work because it dignifies us, Greed and Sloth generated all kinds of scams, greed and theft in the sense that they overburdened people with usury. They lied, saying that such stocks were on the rise when, in fact, they were not, and all that marketing of the big economies do to earn more without effort selling lies.

What pain they caused many families! They damaged the reality of millions of people, but they didn't care. They just wanted to have more from the comfortable seat of their desks.

Then there was the principality of Anger, which strengthened the Sloth; all the strife that the Sloth generated!

All the guilt this generated is for not being efficient and not doing what should be done when it should be done. Sometimes the responsibility did not allow so many human beings to sleep or rest well, all because of laziness, not doing what should be done when it should be done, or not loving work and effort.

What a great mistake their victims fell into! In this way, these four principalities had deceived a large part of the population who obeyed their orders, and if they continued in this way when they died, they would go straight to hell.

Allegria tried to find Costantino's soul in that part of hell. She searched among all that scum. Sometimes she thought she saw him under the clutches of the principality of Pride, Anger or even Sloth. She saw similar faces, but none of them was Costantino.

***

She continued his search and headed north. There was another great principality. Terrifying, worse than the others, however, on a scale equal to the others.

The principality of "Envy" was different from the others. It acted from the shadows; it could not be seen. It was in the dark. However, it suddenly attacked the other principalities as if trying to destroy them from the shadows, just as envy does on Earth.

The funny thing is that they hate each other so much. It is as if they were united by evil, hatred and darkness, by their worship of the devil. However, they cannot destroy each other because they are all connected to doing evil and torturing souls.

Under this principality were souls full of envy who were never satisfied with their position and what they had achieved, always wanting to get, obtain, and be more.

Constant dissatisfaction was their characteristic, as well as criticism, competition and the excessive desire to be the best in everything, no matter the cost, never settling for second place but only longing and doing whatever it took to get first place.

They wanted to have all the spotlights on, to be the most seen and admired by everyone else.

They idolised themselves, idolised and elevated themselves to the status of gods. They thought they deserved the admiration and praise of everyone else.

"Envy" was at work destroying others, preventing others from getting where they wanted to go and putting constant obstacles in the way of others. It was a nightmare.

It's when you can never reach your goal because one or two people are blocking your way. Can you imagine having to deal with that all the time? What a disgrace! That is how envy works; only God can deliver us from such torment.

Envy causes murders. Because there are homicides of all kinds, there are physical homicides that sadly happen. However, there are moral homicides, of the soul, of the spirit, when a person is morally killed to prevent him from reaching something he yearns for, or when the soul of that person is destroyed so that it never reaches its destination; this is how many people fall into deep and great sadness, or what is worse when the spirit of that person is killed so that it never again resurfaces and only sinks into a depression never to see a light of hope again.

When this happens, it is because the spirit of that person is broken, and then he does not even have the strength to try again; he lets himself be finished because he has already come to believe that he is finished. That's breaking a person's spirit and eliminating someone's life.

Yes, there are many ways to commit homicide and evil proceeds through envy to kill good people, righteous, spiritually correct, and with healthy souls, making the blows so strong that these souls are so frustrated that they do not even want to try again. That's how envy works. That's how jealousy gets rid of God's good children.

Of course, there is an almighty God who can keep us from such attacks, but that does not mean that sometimes the good ones do not receive some of them. The good ones also face hardships and hurt a lot when they arrive.

"Envy" may seem harmless, but it is the most lethal; after all, it was the principality used to destroy Jesus. Jesus was perfect and had no sin, error, or malice, but the religion of that day gave him up out of envy. "For he knew that for envy they had delivered him" (Matthew 27.18). Notice how harmful the jealousy he ended up leaving on a cross as the most integral and innocent being that has ever existed in this universe can be.

Envy is dangerous and lethal, it was used to attack Jesus and led him to death on a terrible cross, but thank God, Jesus was not defeated. No one could beat the true Sovereign, Almighty.

***

Allegria was still looking for Costantino all over that infernal compound. She wanted to get out of there but didn't want to go out alone; she wanted Costantino to accompany her and get out of hell together.

Costantino was possessed by unclean spirits that constantly tormented him; the last time she saw him. Still, until now, she could not find him anywhere in that tomb of evil, and Allegria did not know which principality possessed Costantino's soul.

She kept looking, but time was running out because she would transform herself into everything around her if she stayed there. She didn't want that. She was a daughter of God; she wanted to write her destiny in heaven; she knew she belonged to heaven, and she did not want to be stuck in those traps of evil and depravity.

She knew that she couldn't stay in that place much longer. She had to find him quickly, or else she would have to go out alone because staying in that place would mean being trapped by the darkness surrounding her and never being able to get out again. Hence, she decided to hurry out of all that literal hell as soon as possible.

Costantino saw Allegria but ran away from her because he knew that joining Allegria would mean abandoning all the sins he had already adored by then. Costantino may even have been afraid of Allegria because he realized that God was watching over her and helping her to win battles by resisting hell, while God had already abandoned him.

Why did God help Allegria win battles? Until that moment, Allegria had seen and faced the principalities of Pride, Greed, Anger, Sloth, and Envy and had not been defeated; she kept escaping from those influences constantly.

That frightened Costantino because he was so weak that at the first temptation, he gave in; he gave in repeatedly until he became the monster that he was. In other words, he already enjoyed that hell because his sins had seared him entirely. Allegria was the complete opposite of Costantino; while Allegria was wise and strong, Costantino was so foolish, weak and stupid.

Allegria won all her confrontations before these principalities because God helped her; without God's help, all this would have been impossible. Allegria won because she submitted to God, obeying His law, resisted the evil one, and did not subjugate herself before them; evil came, and she fought against it. Then the exhausted wicked one left her for a while; by then, she had defeated those five principalities, and now she had to face the others.

The world admired Allegria; they respected her because they could not understand why she had not fallen under the clutches of some demonic principality until that moment. Allegria was imperfect; she had many defects and weaknesses like any human, but she repented and did not let those forces influence her. She sought to please God and thus remained immune to such destructive forces.

She knew how to fight. Every time she faced giants, she did not go alone; she went with God's anointing as King David would have done when he answered all the insults to Goliath.

"David said to the Philistine: 'You come against me with sword and spear and javelin, but I come against you in the name of the LORD Almighty, the God of the armies of Israel, whom you have defied. This day the LORD will deliver you into my hands, and I'll strike you down and cut off your head. This very day I will give the carcasses of the Philistine army to the birds and the wild animals, and the whole world will know that there is a God in Israel. All those gathered here will know that it is not by sword or spear that the LORD saves; for the battle is the LORD'S, and he will give all of you into our hands" (1 Samuel 17:45-47).

LORD'S was the confidence from Allegria's soul as she faced each battle. That's why she was winning.

She was excellent in some ways but was humble, and she had her heart in heaven and her feet on the ground, in her own words.

Allegria was indestructible because God was with her. Time after time, Costantino saw that God was protecting Allegria and was very afraid of all this because Costantino from hell could observe Allegria and saw her with a protective halo.

Allegria, in turn, proved to be smarter than everyone else. More cunning and intelligent than all the advisors, Costantino heard; even better, Allegria won in the attacks and resisted courageously. That's why her name grew more considerable in heaven and hell. That's truly brave of God's army; she was a heroine.

Allegria was brave and had a big heart; she tried to find Costantino to escape hell but could not find him.

Seeking to find Costantino, she continued to walk in hell as she descended deeper into misery. Suddenly she hears, "Allegria, Allegria!".

Every second she heard her name louder, turned around and saw Costantino; she opened her eyes more intensely, looked at him with amazement, and was stunned.

Costantino and Allegria were both on earth, he asked her where she had been, and he acted usual, she was petrified, she couldn't believe everything she had seen, and at that moment she couldn't understand what she saw was the place where people were building their lives with the decisions they were making, whether in heaven or hell.

She understood that Costantino was getting lost and that he belonged on the other side. Because while she was building her life in heaven, he was making him in hell.

That's when she came to understand everything. They were opposites. He belonged to evil. It was hard for her to regain her composure and act like nothing was happening. She was frozen inside.

Costantino secretly belonged to hell. He had another life that no one knew about, making him belong to hell. Costantino did not understand what was happening with Allegria, but she could see where his life was going.

She tried to keep her composure and behave like nothing was going wrong, but then she broke up. She knew he and she couldn't be together anymore.

They both left the house, he offered to take her back to her home, and they prepared to leave, but she was gone. She had lived in the supernatural world in fractions of a second and understood everything. She was in that parallel world, in that eternal world and where Costantino's soul was besieged. She was absorbed; she had seen the other world. Deep in her heart, she knew they couldn't be together anymore.

Chapter 8
"The sad souls of those who lived without blame and without praise".
Dante Alighieri

Everything had changed. Allegria could no longer continue to act normal with Costantino; she wouldn't date him any more, and no more going out for coffee; she decided to stop kissing and hugging; there was nothing else to do together. To be honest, Allegria was no longer the same; she had begun to repulse Costantino's life, but because of love, she did not want to leave him; this was when he needed her the most.

They do not say that love covers a multitude of sins. Allegria was ready to cover the tons of sins inserted into Costantino's life. Maybe the problem wasn't the sins; the problem was that he didn't want to change, and he was unwilling to give up on evil.

We all do our best to be accepted by the people we care about and want to have in our lives.

One day Costantino decided to ask Allegria out with friends. It was a formal dinner at Kevin's house, Costantino's friend. She wore her best dress, wanting to make a good impression and be accepted by this intimate circle of friends.

So Allegria put on her tenderest pink outfit, body toning cut, a little long, with spaghetti straps, as it was worn in the famous nineties. He picks her up and tells her she is cute, but that's all. They arrive at the place, which looks crowded. There are all kinds of people, and Costantino begins introducing Allegria to new people and new friendships.

They all seemed to emerge alphabetically: Adalia, Agneta, Albert, Emil, Heller, Helmuth, Jenell, Kasch, Leopold, Roth, and Rudolph, among others. They looked like friendly people; they had come from Germany to visit Costantino.

His friends were well-to-do but normal because they were not from such wealthy and influential families as Costantino's. Still, it must be that Allegria was so sensitive to everything that had happened that she was uncomfortable with all those people, and Allegria didn't like those friends because she thought that maybe those friends were pushing him more towards evil.

The friends seemed normal, but they were hellish, all the evil and the damage they caused; they were like people who went down the path of self-destruction and loved their lives to be like that, downhill.

They got high and drank alcohol until they got blasted. Promiscuity was the use, but if it were just promiscuity, they would allow same-sex intercourse and all kinds of evil; however, when the light goes off at night, the orgies would become the carnality feast.

Allegria knew this; she sensed that everything about them was so crooked that it was hard for her to smile at "those new friends".

Allegria wouldn't be part of something like this, but she couldn't understand how Costantino could love and enjoy such an atmosphere. Costantino was delighted with that kind of company, and this made Allegria think that perhaps, after all, it seems that "he is one of them" as the saying goes: birds of the feathers flock together.

That night was a formal dinner; different types of meats, salads, and pasta were served. The dessert table looked splendid with various delicacies, macarons, tiramisu, chocolate cake, flan, cheesecake, brownies with ice cream, a floating island and several other desserts.

Allegria enjoyed dinner, and she knew how to show off her best smile, but once dinner was over, everyone went into the living room to have coffee; well, in fact, she was the only one who was drinking a cup of coffee; the rest from the very first moment had been drinking all kinds of liquor, wine, beer, and some other things.

She doesn't want to bother, so she whispers to Costantino, that she wanna leave because she doesn't feel very comfortable, but he looks at her in awe and asks her: "What do you mean? You don't feel comfortable! This is the best place in the world, honey!". Allegria replies, "Excuse me!", when she said that sentence, there was a resounding silence in the room; Costantino got up from his chair and said, "Sorry, guys, but we have to leave; Allegria feels sick; I think she has the flu or fever."

She became upset, she saw no reason to lie to escape. Once outside, on the sidewalk, she objects, "You don't have to lie; I don't have the flu; I don't have the fever". He grimaces, saying; "I don't understand how you wanna get out of there; we were in the best place in the world, darling! Yeah, that den is my den! Yo, those people I love the most; I love them even more than you!".

Tears rolled from Allegria's eyes, she wanted to cry but held back, so she exclaimed; "Oh God! Costantino! I see; you're one of them; you've become one of them!".

It was as if Allegria was battling against evil; all of them, the so-called Costantino's friends, represented the collapse, and she was alone trying to stand up for what was right, to help Costantino's soul.

That same night Costantino tried to kill all the feelings between them; that night, Costantino had thrown a spear so strong that it destroyed Allegria's heart; it was clear he was no longer the same; he no longer loved her. He loved all the perdition more than God Himself and Allegria. It was as if God and Allegria had lost the soul of Costantino.

***

Considering what Costantino had said, it was like when Saul threw the spear at King David. David had managed to escape no more than in this case; Costantino was even worse than Saul, and Allegria did not feel like David; she felt shocked, weak and powerless, fighting enemies who were much bigger and stronger than her.

A German proverb says, "Fear made the wolf more enormous than it is". Although Allegria was afraid, she knew she was not strong enough to fight against all the evil in which Costantino was immersed.

Allegria turned back and began to walk on the avenue, away from Costantino; tears began to stream down her eyes. She looked to heaven and exclaimed; "God, I think we've lost him; we've already lost him".

God observes all this situation and, as our good God always does, keeps all our tears in His heavenly treasures so that one day, He can return them to us as happiness, blessings, and eternal blissfulness.

At that moment, out of remorse or guilt, we don't know why, Costantino started running after Allegria shouting; "Honey, hold on! Sweetie, please hold on!".

Allegria turns and looks at him and says, "Enough, Costantino, I understood, it's all clear, have a good life, even if the path you are choosing is bad, mean, and perverse. Costantino, there is no good in evil, and you've chosen that: evil!".

When she finished saying that, they were both in hell again. She sees how the demons take Costantino's soul and drag him into hell's depths.

She begins to cry out in desperation, yelling; "Costantino! Where are you going? Where are they taking you?" Demons with bloody claws, full of fangs, horns, and the appearance of monsters, literally monsters that smelled of perversity and sulphur, were still dragging Costantino's soul. Then as she approached, she saw those demons up close and shouted in fear, full of terror; "Roth, Leopold!" They were Costantino's "friends", pretending to be his most significant and close friends, when in reality, they were agents of hell itself sent to destroy Costantino's soul.

Why should we deceive ourselves? Costantino loved these agents of evil more than anything else; he loved to be destroyed by them and kill himself with his so-called friends; they had become essential in his life.

Costantino had abandoned all the good he could enjoy in this society to be with these agents. These agents dragged him into the lava of filth and perversion. Allegria witnessed this collapse of Costantino's soul.

Costantino loved to enjoy the lavas of destruction. Costantino had come to love perversion more than anything else in this world. Costantino had become a perverse being himself. At that moment, Allegria asked herself, as a good Christian, if she should try to get him out of there; it was clear that she was alone and that Costantino would never leave this hell again.

In that situation, out of compassion and mercy, she tried to warn Costantino one last time of the path he was taking, but she knew she had to hurry because she could not stay there for long.

***

Suddenly, Allegria opened her eyes and was absorbed like never before because the worst principalities were showcasing themselves to her. All principalities are equally evil and perverse, but these were the most powerful ones in favour of evil.

Allegria was almost at the bottom of hell; she was in the south of suffering, and now what she could see would be the worst thing a human being could see in his whole life and for eternity. Moreover, the eyes of the human being are not prepared to see so much hatred, evilness, and concentrated perversion, but there was the soul of Costantino, loving all that filth.

Allegria knew they were heading south of hell. The first thing she saw was a vast principality: giant, deformed, sometimes thin, skinny, sometimes fat, occasionally anorexic, sometimes bulimic, sometimes excessively fat, sometimes overweight, and sometimes rickety. His mouth was shattered, his teeth were bleeding, and he used scissors to cut his mouth, making it bigger, then he used thread and needle to sew it up, making it tiny; it was the principality of "Gluttony" of disorders; disorder of excessive desires.

Now this principality was not isolated; it was accompanied by the principality of "Lust," this principality provoked total exaltation of the body; it was surrounded by fire, it burned and groaned with pain, but its most significant concern was to appear desirable to the masses, everyone wanted that principality, it was wild sex personified.

Just as Jesus is love personified, no one is sweeter and better than Jesus. "Lust" is the opposite. It was desire and perversion embodied.

The principality of "Lust" had exuberant breasts, had a tremendous emphasis on the butt, on the way it was moved, focused on the muscles, the shape of the body, it also focused on the male sexual organ, on its immensity, it was a hermaphrodite; sometimes a man, sometimes a woman. It switches according to how it wants to manifest itself; its most excellent followers were the men who dressed up and acted as women. With that sensualism, those sensual movements drive the masses wild.

The masses were screaming because they thought it was fun and unique. Apart from these men who acted as women, their other faithful followers were the courtesan women, women who wanted to drive the male masses mad about their bodies, their seduction, and their pornographic poses; these women loved this principality and followed and served it with all the strength of their hearts.

They, the courtesans, were used to bring destruction to society, as they used charms with diabolical doses to drive men crazy and make them forget to be good husbands loving their wives, to go on to be with their wives but being charmed by these courtesans.

They were mean-spirited women, but their perversion made them so subtle that they seemed not to harm society when they did the worst damage because they destroyed families.

Many men forgot their covenant before God to love and be faithful to their wives, and they ended up admiring, desiring, and coveting these women. In fact, inside these women operated a Jezebel spirit because they seduced and enchanted men to incite them to evil, thus abandoning goodness, so men are enslaved before their charms and left the integrity to follow a path of sin that hurt their souls, causing just pain and death.

Death in this century and eternal death, but they didn't seem to care. These men were so foolish!

Now the dose of evil increased when the women used to recreate male fantasies were married women, those women who embarrassed their husbands, and the degree of corruption increased when married men went on to desire this kind of women, which makes adultery exalted at its best. They were repulsive, but they bragged so much they boasted of being the great thing when in reality, all their souls only generated aversion because they were so perverse and decadent. They fail to realize the harm they did to themselves, their families, and their children!

Maybe at that moment, Allegria should have been merciful and asked God to save them, but in reality, Allegria proceeded as a simple human and exclaimed to God: "O Lord, why don't you finish them all now? They are so decadent!" To which God replied, "My mercy renews itself every morning, my sweet daughter".

These principalities operated together, "Gluttony" and "Lust" were amalgamated. Gluttony consists of "wanting more". For gluttony, "nothing is ever enough," and lust is practically the same; none of those souls under the influence of these principalities felt satisfied, so they fell into descending wells.

This well began with fornication; fornication always takes its pleasure in contaminating the purest soul; in other words, fornication went after the virgins and the very young who were still chaste; they wanted the bodies of the virgins or chaste ones to contaminate them in this way. Nonetheless, it is not harmful to be a virgin, but the important thing is to turn this virginity or chastity into an offering under the blessing of God in marriage.

God always made a covenant using blood to seal that covenant; God with Abraham through the sacrifice of animals, God with humanity through Jesus, God closes a marriage between a man and a woman at that very moment when the woman offers her virginity as an oblation, because she sheds blood, and there at that moment the covenant is sealed; those two souls are united forever.

That is why the enemy of our souls is so interested in women being promiscuous that there is no covenant so that no such covenant is made. The enemy of our souls wants all women to be vulgar and go into marriage, having come from a long list of experiences so she is no longer oblivious to the fact that a man and woman have to seal a covenant with the blessed of God having their first sexual intercourse.

This world has become so rampant because we have forgotten the proper ways, the ancient paths, the right way to walk, and the decent way to do everything.

In short, that was the infernal reality, to ruin the virgins, if possible, all the virgins of the planet so that the covenant would not become concrete and nothing would become valid and accurate on this earth.

After fornication, there was adultery. More destructive forces of evil were operating there; it was pure iniquity, sin, and perversion, which destroyed homes and families. The affair always works in the same way, promising the world on the other side of the fence, when in reality, by jumping over the wall, all the protection of God is lost and the demons of destruction rule over that soul.

Under the influence of adultery, lust and evil are more powerful; both are at fault, the person who is desired and the one who wants. It causes so much harm to so many, it is full of pure selfishness, narcissism at its best, and it is the desire for the greater self. It was to forget God's commandments and decide with total rebellion the path one wanted to take.

Many women intentionally fornicate to profit from the other person; of course, both please each other. Inherently, both of them are doomed to hell, but they consider this way as a way of climbing into this society.

They are willing to do everything for the sake of achieving their personal goals, and many men have fallen into adultery in search of more wild pleasure; that is, these men aren't aligned with the responsibility of loving and caring for their wives, but they narcissistically decide that they deserved more, that they owe to have more, so they go for it and got it; being utterly oblivious that as husbands they have to learn to sacrifice their desires for their wives.

In adultery, the evil empire operated; the famous lie rules here: "Since my spouse does not give me what I want, I will seek it in another way". He was the "I" at the highest level, forgetting the "we" and the sacrifice of serving others, such as the spouse, the children, and the family.

Then when perversion was on the rise, it descended into homosexuality and lesbianism; men acted as women, women as men and gender identity had been lost, and it was a perverse point. Allegria had seen all that and couldn't take it anymore and started vomiting; she puked everything in her stomach; she shuddered; those people were like they were no longer people; they were so malformed that they looked like demons.

These people wanted society to approve of what they were doing at all costs; they wanted society to accept all these unrestrained means, and they wanted the organization to support them to calm their consciences because deep down, they knew that this was something that God would never accept.

God is a perfect being who created each being with a specific function, the man to be a true man and the woman to be a true lady. These people were pitiful. They weren't happy. They were tormented. When everything deviated so abruptly, they went against themselves from the function and role God endowed humanity with.

It was so nasty to see what they had become, and at times, they enjoyed their sins, but then depression, guilt, and loneliness overwhelmed them. They needed so much alcohol and drugs to soften their consciences, to soften the torment that haunted them.

Although the voice of their consciences was becoming increasingly silent, they still knew in their hearts that they were wrong. Still, so much hatred and rebellion consumed them that they hated God, the church, and everyone, especially the pastors who preached against such sin.

The rebellion in all areas was evident in them. They have rebelled against God's plan for their lives. Then, how could they be pleased? It's impossible. We have no goodness outside of God; we cannot be satisfied without forgetting God's ways.

***

That descending section was the filth section, but it was not the only one; there were more degrees of perversion as it went down into the depths of hell; it got worse; there was the child abuse section; they were natural agents of evil to pervert a child's innocence and harm their lives forever.

Then followed the incest section, which destroys families, trust, and healthy relationships; part of this was also the zoophilia section.

Such were the wild desires for lust, gluttony, and a wild sexual appetite that some people ate their faecal matter to feed their wildest desires. There were orgies and drunkenness everywhere in this section. It was a filthy area.

Imagine the consequences: more liquor, more food, more pleasure, more sensuality, more of everything, all in excess.

People who were chained to these perversions were on their way to hell; though at first enjoyed them, once sin was over, there was guilt, pain, anguish, and remorse, and it was so hard for them even to breathe because no human being was created to live in that state. Every human being was created to have a dignified and honourable life, a relationship with God, follow His principles and develop a righteous and good life. That's the foundation where true happiness lies, in being able to wake up in the morning, make a cup of coffee, give a smile to your parents, have a spouse who loves you, obedient children, share lunch around a family table every Sunday, in celebrating the small delights of life, such as meeting your grandmother and going for a walk in a park. That is life, the enjoyment of small details, as Paul would say in his letter to the Romans: "For the kingdom of God is not eating and drinking, but righteousness and peace and joy". In other words, by doing the right thing, we find peace, and happiness.

When one understands that by living with simplicity and humility, one becomes happy, it is when God's children rejoice in heavenly happiness. One is pleased to see the children playing, to be able to enjoy a walk, to swim in the pool, to have coffee and toast for breakfast, to have a warm blanket on cold nights, to see the sun, to hear the children leaving school, watching the young people play a football match, being able to kiss the people you love, feeling your mother's hand on your hand, hugging your friends, family, and a loving pet... Yes, knowing and feeling how much love one gets and how much can be given to others genuinely matter.

After all, one will not take anything from this earth into eternity, only the goodness that one has given to others. For the kingdom of God does not consist in material gain, but in doing the will of God, and to be truly happy, we must be part of that kingdom; and in obeying His words, we find our destiny, we come to understand what we were created for, the seeds of love we must spread on this earth.

By understanding His kingdom, we know our hearts, and why we are the way we are. With God, everything makes sense; even our unique personality has a reason for being within His kingdom.

Within all that hell, Allegria observes that Costantino is amid all those souls who served lust. She felt agape love, a heavenly love that caused her pain seeing Costantino in that situation while trying to save him. Allegria was devastated seeing him in that situation, and by that time, she had no romantic feelings towards him; by that time, her feelings turned to mercy and pity when she saw the state of Costantino's soul.

At that moment, Allegria calls him; "Costantino, Costantino!" She runs towards him and says: "Costantino, you must get out of here; this is hell, literal hell. Costantino, you deserve the best for your life, get out of here, run away, run away with me. I think we still have time to save ourselves!".

Costantino was possessed by so much evil that he shouted at her; "Stay away from me! If you come back and try to save me again, I'll kill you". Allegria replied, "Costantino, it's your soul that's at stake; please don't get lost". Full of evil, Costantino groaned; "Go away and don't ever come back; I don't want to hear from you any more".

The look of hatred in Costantino's eyes indicated it was all over. Costantino was lost and already loved evil, with no desire to repent.

Allegria understands that he has already decided to get lost, so she decides to leave the place immediately. She was heartbroken but agreed that Costantino's bad decisions would not affect her. Emotionally she was devastated, but rationally she decided that this would not sink her and that she would come out of there from where Costantino had dragged her since she did not belong there.

A herd of souls surrounded by fire, worms, and with their skin infested with rot rushed towards Allegria at great speed.

***

She manages to wipe away the tears that had caused her such a situation and decides to run to get out of there; the herd was approaching and pushing her to the worst place, to the place where nobody humanly wanted to be, but where all those who had rejected Jesus were, in the very centre of hell.

The souls infested with sin live in hell; they have no peace, everything is anguish, torment, deformation, perversion… and there they were all in the centre of hell worshipping the great beast, all there serving Satan, he hated, tortured, mocked and destroyed them, but they loved being beaten by Satan. They loved being part of such a sick relationship.

While the relationship with Jesus is constructive, peaceful, and healthy, following Satan produces the opposite.

Curiously, we worry when we have the flu and rush to the doctor for a prescription for some aspirin to be cured. Still, when our soul is sick, we do not run to the Doctor of doctors so that our soul may heal, being that He alone has the remedy that our soul needs: His love and His forgiveness.

The centre of hell was madness; all hell was a nightmare, but the centre of hell was something infinitely worse.

It was like a great feast conducted by the principality of Idolatry; everyone worshipped the beast. It was horror, darkness, perversion, and pain at its best, and everyone raised their hands and danced madly. If any of these souls became exhausted, the demons beat him, stuck spears in them so that none of these souls would stop and continue dancing to please the beast.

Allegria could no longer breathe from the oppression she felt and prayed to God to get her out of there.

These souls who lay in such a place of hell had entered this system for fun, but now they were tired, fed up, and corrupted; they saw no reason for what they were doing, and even when they wanted to stop, they could no longer. As the music played, it altered all their senses, and it seemed they were getting deeper.

Souls in the real world need to get high to experience all that world of sensations, but in hell, souls didn't need drugs or alcohol; all their senses were at ten thousand per cent; souls cried, closed their eyes, raised their hands, it was true worship, but they couldn't stop, so they had to keep moving in everlasting adoration to the beast.

There were no fireworks to welcome you there; the fire was real; there were no drugs to alter your senses and make you experience other sensations; there, all your feelings were at their maximum, and no matter how much you wanted to stop feeling, you could no longer do so... you were already inside, and there was no emergency exit.

All souls were suffocated, weary and tired, but they did not want to stop serving the devil. Can the human heart be so complex that it still loves rebellion, knowing it is on its way to destruction? Why would human beings love self-destruction? Why not turn to goodness, righteousness, honour, and dignity?

Allegria just thought about getting out of there; she couldn't stand that place any longer; in fractions of a second, the site seemed unbearable with everything she had seen. Can you imagine what it would be like to live there for eternity?

***

Allegria started running to get out as soon as possible, but the darkness was getting thicker; she was entering the witchcraft, the witches' section, where everyone wanted to do their will.

They performed some witchcraft to get what they wanted, not realizing that in doing so, they only attracted curses for their lives because they got something, sometimes. Still, they had to pay so painfully for everything they had achieved that, for a moment, they had the satisfaction of achieving it, but still, the torment was constant.

All those who consulted the horoscopes, those who read cards, those who read coffee beans, those who cast their luck, and so many others have fortune tellers because they wanted to know the future without asking the true God.

The people in that section were rebelliously looking for different means to know the future, which they managed to find out, but in a distorted way, because of lies and deceit. The evil spirits manipulated their lives so that certain things could happen.

It is terrible to be in error because nothing you are living is true; deception is destructive because you build your world upon lies.

Sometimes some people play with this world of darkness and open themselves up to horror movies, satanic music, and satanic cartoons; everything seems just like a game, and in this way, their lives begin to be infested, they fall into depression, things don't start to work out for them, they seem cursed, everything goes wrong, and then they wonder why nothing can ever go right for them, why nothing seems to work for them.

When someone is far from God's will and open to that world of darkness, the curse is automatically upon their lives; it's like the devil gives him what needs not to leave that world, but the darkness doesn't give him enough to be complete or happy, because the devil can't give what he doesn't possess: peace, love, and happiness.

Sorcery operates under the principality of "Idolatry" too; everybody tries to look for another source other than God, the true God.

***

It is time to clean the house; that is to say, to clean the heart, to put in order what must be ordered and to take out everything cursed from our lives.

Everything that does not serve God serves the darkness, and we cannot be half-hearted in this; we serve God or the devil. We cannot serve two masters because we will please one and offend the other.

Everything in our life that does not please God must be eradicated. We must choose who we will serve and who we will please, whether it be God or the darkness; walking half-heartedly is the worst sin we can commit.

Today is a great day to choose and abandon evil at once and only serve God himself.

In that section of hell, there were covenants, with blood, with sacrifice, whether of one's blood or animals, even human sacrifices of babies, children, and virgin women. It was the terrifying section, and what is worse, all those souls mocked God, the church, and the pastors; they wanted to finish them with all their hearts and eradicate them from the face of the earth; their plan was "that it be on earth as it is in hell", without churches, without pastors; so everybody will end up worshipping the beast.

In that part of the principality of "Idolatry", Allegria was astonished to see the section of heresy, all those who had served deception. That section was very subtle because pastors and churches in hell still supposedly did God's will but went after the money and preached all kinds of lies, false theories, and arguments. They taught something that seemed genuine but was mistaken; they are known as "false prophets". They use a truth but distort it so that it becomes a hoax.

The Holy Bible has already warned us in the second letter Paul wrote to Timothy in chapter three: "But mark this: There will be terrible times in the last days. People will be lovers of themselves, lovers of money, boastful, proud, abusive, disobedient to their parents, ungrateful, unholy, without love, unforgiving, slanderous, without self-control, brutal, not lovers of the good, treacherous, rash, conceited, lovers of pleasure rather than lovers of God— having a form of godliness but denying its power. Have nothing to do with such people. They are the kind who worm their way into homes and gain control over gullible women, who are loaded down with sins and are swayed by all kinds of evil desires, always learning but never able to come to a knowledge of the truth. Just

as... opposed Moses, these teachers also opposed the truth. They are men of depraved minds who are rejected as far as the faith is concerned. But they will not get very far because, as in the case of those men, their folly will be clear to everyone".
We must be careful not to fall into deception. We must follow the whole truth and walk in the truth.

***

Once upon a time, in a London airport, a drug dealer was arrested, and when the police took the computer away from the drug dealer, the drug leader said: "It is useless; you will not have proof of my actions because I erased all the transactions". Police officers took the computer to a specialist at the factory that manufactured these computers. They could recover everything erased from their memory, enough to arrest the drug trafficker and give him 20 years in prison.
The world does not understand that one day everybody will be returned to the Manufacturer, and everything we have done, said, watched, or heard has gone to the human subconscious. God has access to that information and will get it out; Jesus said: "For there is nothing hidden that will not be concealed that will not be known or brought out into the open".
The tragic thing about today's evangelisation methods is the way they are exposed is that they make the gospel look like an apparent business, like a commercial transaction.
Today's way differs significantly from how the true gospel was presented for two thousand years, as Jesus, Paul, and great preachers like Spurgeon, Wesley, and men who preached the truth.
What happens is that modern evangelists have decided not to address conscience because it does not want to make a person feel guilty, it does not want to offend him, so it goes on to say things that encourage the desire for happiness instead of showing them

their sin and letting their consciences make them cry out to a merciful God.

They speak of sin in a general and arbitrary way, removing personal responsibility.

Jesus, Paul, and even the prophet Nathan addressed personal responsibility aimed at people's consciences. We can do the same through God's commandments and moral standards to show how wrong our acts might be and that if we continue on that path, we will have trouble on the day of judgment before God, so we become aware of how desperately we need God's forgiveness.

***

Imagine a child cutting their leg off with a piece of rusty tin; their mother takes the child to the doctor, and they would say: "This child needs tetanus shot right above the wound; he won't like it, so I'll give him some candy; he might die, but I have pleased him". Of course, that wouldn't happen in real life; what the doctor will tell her is something like, "Hold your child tightly; I'll put tetanus shot right in the wound; he'll hate you, and he'll hate me, but he'll save his life."

Suppose we genuinely love the lost ones, those who are on their way to hell, we would expose God's law as if we stick a needle to penetrate the flesh, it will hurt them, but this will raise their awareness towards their sins, bring them knowledge and show them that they have sinned against God. In that case, that is how the saving liquid of the gospel can do its work.

Spurgeon said that the Christian who was so afraid of offending and being rejected by others that he didn't tell them anything, like a doctor who has a remedy but doesn't help the patient because he fears that the bad news that the person is sick will make him unwilling to listen. We must tell the ill person that they are sick.

Spurgeon said, "You're too delicate to tell the man he's sick. You expect to heal the illness without them knowing it. Therefore, you flatter them. So what's going on? They're laughing at you. They dance on their graves and finally die. Your delicacy is cruelty; your flattery is poison, and you're a murderer. Will we lock men up in the fool's Paradise? Lull them into a sweet sleep from which they'll awaken in hell? Collaborate in their damnation with our soft speeches? For God's sake, we must not do so".

The medicine tastes bitter but is effective, and sometimes, sadly, what has happened is that they have diluted the gospel to take away the bitterness to have a sweeter taste but make it lose its healing properties.

The message has been softened to appeal to the sinner, removing bitterness, such as references to righteousness, judgment, sin, and the Ten Commandments. This is serious, and all the people who had deviated from the true doctrine, the sound teachings, the true gospel by deceiving themselves to benefit themselves and not the sinner, all of them once dead, were in this section of heresy inside hell because they had given in to the truth and only taught deception along with lies.

The souls that had followed these false leaders were also there; they were in charge of torturing them while hellish forces tortured them.

***

The church is the bride of Christ, and all believers are part of that body called "the church". As the bride, the church has the function of exalting the bridegroom, living in the way that pleases God, sharing the faith and not forgetting to do mercy.

In this hedonistic, narcissistic, and selfish century, where everything focuses on "personal gain" or "personal empires", we must stop all such influences and live as true Christians exercising mercy while sharing the truth.

We need to help others without having a hidden agenda. Where are mercy and compassion? Where are humility and sacrifice?

Mercy is a word that comes from Latin, "miserere", which means compassion and "cor", which means heart. To be merciful is to have a compassionate heart. Mercy, joy, and peace are the effects of love, that is, charity.

To have charity is to express faith in deeds. Mercy is divided into spiritual compassion and bodily mercy. Spiritual understandings are: to teach the unlearned, to give good advice to those who need it, to correct those who err, to forgive the injury, to console the sad, to endure the weaknesses of others, and to pray for others.

The corporal mercies are: to feed the hungry, give drink to the thirsty, provide shelter to the pilgrim, clothe the naked, visit the sick people, help the captive, and bury the dead. Mercy must come upon us to care for widows and orphans, help street children, care for people experiencing homelessness, and teach those who do not know so that they can come out of ignorance; in that and many other ways, one can show mercy.

When another person is suffering or struggling, mercy must come upon us. Mercy must be the emblem of our faith.

Faith is demonstrated in deeds. If you care for and help your neighbour, you confirm that you are a faithful follower of Jesus. Faith is sometimes seen in silence, whether with their spiritual or physical needs.

Faith is simple, in doing something for others but with a pure heart, without asking anything in return. Do something for someone who can't pay you back. Do everything without hidden intentions. That is the purity of faith. That is true faith; to walk in love, to put an attachment to others. Faithful followers of Jesus must walk in love, which is the perfect bond.

Faith is simple. It is to help one's neighbour, to share with others, it is to serve, it is to be generous, it is to be unselfish, it is not to focus on oneself, but to focus on God and on what one can give and serve others.

The people who lay in hell in the heresy section had forgotten mercy and loved only money, personal achievement and the creation of empires in their name. It was total chaos because they used the most sacred thing: "faith" for personal gain.

Allegria saw all this, and her heart was broken; she had already seen more in seconds than she had ever wanted to see in her entire life. She was exhausted from seeing so much evil; everything in hell seemed like a great feast but a dinner towards destruction. So astonished from observing so much damage, without a second of peace or respite, she lifted her eyes up and away as in another galaxy. She saw that there was heaven; all that surrounded that world was peace, glory, light, splendour, and so much joy.

There everyone appreciated, respected, and loved each other. There was no wickedness, evil intentions, or hidden jealousy, and she could even see entire families belonging to heaven. Looking up at heaven from hell, she could see that a father looked after his wife and loved his children; the woman was virtuous and looked after her family; the children were happy and obeyed their parents; everything was harmonious, balanced, peaceful, and gentle. It was another galaxy; it was heaven.

From hell, she could see how many families were in heaven, healthy, happy, gentle, obedient, and respectful youngsters. She could see two brothers walking their grandmother, a young woman waking up, having coffee in the morning and praying to God for the new day.

She saw teenagers riding their bikes to school; they were all gentle and well-treated and knew how to treat each other with love; other young people played football and did not misbehave. She saw young ladies preparing a picnic and sharing constructive conversations; they did not criticize or make fun of anyone but encouraged each other in the different endurance tests they faced.

They were people who were building their lives to spend eternity with Jesus. They were people who here on earth did not choose evil but good, which is why their lives were being built in heaven. It was Paradise.

It's incredible, but from hell, they can watch the people in heaven torture them; it's a constant reminder of everything you've lost. Perhaps that is their greatest torment, not the devil himself, but seeing what they missed because they have rejected Jesus.

***

How foolish human beings can be to abandon goodness to follow evil! Incredible but true, some people seemed born to love the darkness, and others have wisely decided to love God and His principles. The people who were on their way to heaven were people who had decided to love God here on earth.

Suddenly she saw a young man dressed as a kind, gentle, and educated prince helping his father work in a newspaper and book printing press. He was a young aspiring, enterprising and hard-working man. He was sweet in his treatment of others. At that moment, Allegria's heart woke up and longed to be there, to see so much love, sweetness, good treatment, all that moved her heart and thought how beautiful it would be to leave behind hell, so much evil, damage and move on to live there, in heaven.

Allegria imagined how beautiful it would be to be treated by a young prince, by an actual prince, a man of goodness… and in that moment of so much affliction, she longed to be there, in heaven, in Paradise. She longed for one day to be with a young man like that, with a heavenly young man, because she was tired of so much chaos, evil and hell.

She looked down, and all she could think of was: "I have to get out of here". She wanted to leave all that hell behind. She started running and looking for a way out of that pit of despair, and in her anguish, she cried out to God and said: "Please don't leave me, get me out of here, get me out of here forever. Never let me come back to this place, never let me come back again!".

At that moment, Allegria bent down to pray amid all that hell and putting her hands together, she remembered two verses she had learned as a child and implored God to fulfil them in her life: "God, please, 'He lifted me out of the slimy pit, out of the mud admire; he set my feet on a rock and gave me a firm place to stand Psalm 40.2'. And please, God, have mercy on me and 'who redeems your life from the pit and crowns you with love and compassion' Psalm 103.4'. God, I know I deserve nothing, but please do not let me go out of this hell, take me out of here, have mercy on me and take me out of here".

By saying that prayer Allegria was not demanding justice; she was crying out for mercy; she felt like the tax collector who went to the temple to ask God for forgiveness and not like the Pharisee who demanded justice as if she had the right to get out of there.

She understood how sinful she was and that only God's mercy would allow her to come out of that hell which was so coarse, extensive, and immense, where so many people were going to destruction.

***

She looked into the depths of that hell, feeling discouraged, depressed, and worse still, without the hope that she would ever get out of it. It was such a deep well that humanly, she would never be able to climb to the surface; she was unable to go out of there, nor in billions of years would she be able to build a ladder to even reach the edge of the surface of hell. So she just closed her eyes and waited, crying to God, asking him for mercy and letting her out of there.

***

Costantino shakes Allegria, and she returns to the real world; they are in the street where the argument had started and in a few seconds, she saw everything, understood everything, understood the hell in which Costantino lived and saw all the future that would await her if she stayed next to him.

She saw the corruption for the first time in Costantino's eyes.

Allegria shook and stopped Costantino from touching her. She had understood that it was time to split apart, that he belonged to hell, but she was part of heaven. She would live next to him in agony because his whole life was hell, and she didn't want that.

Allegria wanted, in the real world, to pack her things and go as far away from him as possible; she felt that in all that time, he had just been chewing her and then just spat at her.

His mouth was poisoned, and he had taken only the good stuff from her and was done with her, but no more; she was determined to eliminate all this nightmare.

Allegria had seen heaven; she had seen the perfection, the happiness, the joy; she had seen that there are better people on this planet. She had decided that she wanted someone who belonged to heaven, to the place where she belonged, because she was determined to get out of that hell, the hell of despair, the miry clay, that hell called reality into which Costantino had introduced her, making her live in constant affliction.

She looks at Costantino with eyes of compassion, exhaustion, tiredness, and as if it were the last time she would see him. She was already determined to let him go forever.

Costantino takes her hand and understands that everything has changed. She drops a tear and says to him; "Costantino, I tried to save you; it was love, no one can deny it, there in the hell we live in, I tried to rescue you, I tried to destroy your walls, but in reality, it was you who broke me, I tried to lift you to heaven, but you always pushed me into hell, you slowly burned me with your flames".

Allegria sighed as she tried to raise her eyes to heaven because it was hard to express what she was feeling; she looked at him again and kept telling him with determination, "But you will no longer be able to break the last thing that is left of me, you will not be able to take my soul, you won't ever take this from me, I belong to heaven, and I want to say goodbye forever! I hate my reality. I can not live a lie, running to find a solution to all this; I let you go because you loved the darkness more than the light, so this is the end".

Allegria tries to wipe away all the tears on her cheeks. Costantino was also weeping at the time.

Costantino understood that this was a goodbye, that there would be no turning back, that she was letting him go forever.

Costantino babbles softly: "Yes, I understand that I made you go through hell because I am part of that hell. Forgive me; if I can say just one thing, it would be: forgive me". Allegria says, "I forgive you, and God will forgive you too if you ask for forgiveness".

Allegria looks down. It was silence between them. Then she starts to let go of Costantino's hand and asks him to let hers go, "Costantino, please, let go of my hand, it's the end, it's over, we've come to the end of all this nightmare, your love was cheap, but I paid dearly for it. I tried everything I could to be with you, but you let me down. Once and a thousand times, you let me down! So take all your lies and deceptions; you can no longer break me; our souls will be separated forever, you are going down, and I am determined to raise my soul again. I saw heaven, Costantino. I want all heaven's beautiful things: a happy and peaceful life".

The tears in both of them run like streams.

Costantino was saying goodbye to the only woman who had shaken him, but at the end of the story, nothing remained. Their souls were separated forever; she began walking upwards while he continued down.

Allegria starts walking on her way home and just passes a music store that is playing sad, melancholy, farewell songs as if to say goodbye. If it were in our decade it would be a song like the one by the band Maná, the song entitled "Tengo muchas alas". Allegria opened her wings and started to fly.

Just what Allegria needed to fly, open her wings and get out of all those circumstances that oppressed her.

Allegria was saying goodbye in her way to the person she had dearly loved, but she was already determined to spread her wings; even if she was thrown down or fell, she was not going to give up; she was determined to get out of the bloody hell to which Costantino had introduced her. She decided to go to heaven and live in heaven, in that heavenly reality, not in that toxic and sickly reality Costantino had introduced her to.

***

It seems that all of heaven and hell knew of their separation because, from hell, the cries of anguish grew louder and louder as Costantino descended.

Instead, the heaven began to shine brighter over Allegria's life; hope was shining over Allegria's eyes, and more light surrounded her. She had more light than ever before.

Costantino was going to the left, downwards, while Allegria had decided to go to the right, and now everything in her life was beginning to shine; little by little more light was descending on her life, and now she was starting to live her true destiny: rise and shine.

It was the end. Costantino's soul continued to descend into the depths of hell where he wanted to belong and felt he belonged, and Allegria's soul began to rise instantly.

Hell grew farther from her reality and, like a meteor, Allegria began to climb upward. She saw that heaven was opening up to her and smiled for the first time in years. Her life was smiling again; she was happy again.

What a decision Allegria had made when she decided to abandon Costantino's life at last, but even though she had come out of the depths of hell, she was still at the well and needed a miracle to get to heaven.

However, miracles do happen, and Allegria is full of hope for what she is waiting for a gift. For a second, she turned her head down and saw Costantino being embraced by his friends, some of them as foolish as he was; Allegria saw that some friends were not friends but were infernal legions that pushed him deeper and deeper down into the depths of hell; but Costantino loved them, he loved that life.

Costantino disappeared into the infernal legions, and Allegria could no longer see him as she continued her ascent. The last thing she saw was demons caressing Costantino's soul, those infected claws full of blood and pus stroked him, and he smiled. She couldn't believe how Costantino took such pleasure in so much evil. That was the last time she saw him. She has already looked up to the sky, full of hope.

She was delighted again, but the best was yet to come, and she started heading towards it, to the best reward ever... heaven itself.

Chapter 9
**"Heaven wheels above you, displaying to you her eternal glories,
and still your eyes are on the ground".
Dante Alighieri**

It had been almost three years. It was 1996. That year was a period of many things happening, such as the assassination of Hamas activist Yahya Ayyash by the Israeli secret services, the demand by UNICEF for urgent explanations from the People's Republic of China for the deaths of thousands of children in orphanages in the country, and another important fact was that the Peruvian writer and politician Mario Vargas Llosa took up the seat of the Royal Spanish Academy.

DNA was introduced into the malaria parasite genome, a significant breakthrough. Also in the same year, the Olympic Games were held in Atlanta, USA, and the European Championship, where Germany won the title after defeating the Czech Republic in the final, which was held in England.

Bill Clinton was re-elected, and as for the art world, it was a year in which good films such as "Fargo", the classics that have prevailed over time such as "The Hunchback of Notre Dame" and "Independence Day", the comedy "The Nutty Professor," and those that received several awards such as "Evita" and "The English Patient" were produced.

It was a year of many alterations and some progress.

That year was crucial for Allegria as her soul was being cleansed. It was a process to get all the hell out of it and let the light penetrate her soul's depths. It took time, and it was not that simple; it was a difficult path to walk through; however, she was grateful because she was determined to get out of the hell and out of all the chaos she had experienced.

She was tired of the whole system that had subjugated her for so long and knew she had to break it. She had begun her freedom and even felt freer as if she had started ascending to heaven, but she was not yet in the place she should and wanted to be.

She felt that she was coming out of hell and on her way to heaven, but she was not yet in heaven, where milk and honey flow, where all the dreams come true, where the greatest joys and true happiness can be experienced.

Hell would not let her go so quickly; it was preparing to give her the counter-attack; the war would be unleashed for her soul, and she would have to be strong and resilient because, with God's help, she would win.

Allegria was at peace in her heart because she knew that God himself would defend her and that He had the most powerful army in the universe, the army of the kingdom of heaven, on her side.

Allegria clung to the Holy Bible, and this increased her wisdom. Reading and meditating on the Holy Bible's words helped her stand on her feet during the problematic seasons she was living while waiting to get entirely out of hell.

Allegria sought to delight in God's promises. This kept her alive as she waited day after day, finally to get out of the way.

Sometimes it was hard for her to endure the day-to-day while she waited for her complete liberation. There were irritable and challenging days. However, she tried to say to herself, "God helps me, I'm strong because God is helping me, I'm going to get out of this, I will see that I will get out of here, I will resist", and in tears, totally exhausted, she fell asleep... she fell asleep inside the hell.

***

Allegria knew that the more she cultivated her relationship with Jesus, the more she nurtured her soul as she meditated on the Holy Bible, on the truths of God, she was renewed, and its interior filled with light.

The light was already with her, she had never been alone, even in the midst of hell, but the light needed to increase to be completely free from the suffering she had lived.

As Allegria grew in intimacy and closeness with her saviour Jesus, her soul got better; it was as if all the knots her soul had ever had were loosened one by one. Jesus, with his wisdom and his time, helped to heal all the wounds.

Allegria was full of peace and rejoiced in that grace, even though she was in hell waiting to come out of the affliction totally. The Holy Bible was her great companion and filled her with understanding.

Allegria dreamed of living in that heaven; she wanted to escape all the nasty things surrounding her. At times she felt afraid, so she would meditate on verses that strengthened her inner self; these were some of her favourites:

"Have I not commanded you? Be strong and courageous. Do not be afraid; do not be discouraged, for the Lord your God will be with you wherever you go" (Joshua 1:9).

"So do not fear, for I am with you; do not be dismayed, for I am your God. I will strengthen you and help you; I will uphold you with my righteous right hand" (Isaiah 41:10).

And one, in particular, gave her hope that she would be free and have a good life after all:

"He will call on me, and I will answer him; I will be with him in trouble, I will deliver him and honor him. With long life I will satisfy him and show him my salvation" (Psalms 91:15 and 16).

Allegria meditated on that phrase repeatedly: "I will deliver him and glorify him" and prayed to the God of heaven to deliver her, to deliver her from all the hell she had been through.

One is unhappy living in a sick society under a corrupted system. Who can be happy like that? But how beautiful is an organisation that fears God, loves goodness and whose citizenship is built on truth!

How beautiful is a society where goodness, morals, and ethics reign! What a lovely face ethics has! Where children play in the parks, young people play sports or attend the reading club, where people ride bikes freely, where children respect their fathers and take care of their mothers.

Where citizens go to church and have good lives, sow only goodness, have principles, and build good families.

Where husbands are faithful to their wives and lead by example in a godly life, where people love work and are willing to work, where wives care for their husbands and lovingly fulfil the needs their children may have.

Where the whole family goes to church and honours God. Where the bus gives way to the ladies in the first place, where the newspaper is responsible for telling the truth and not selling sensationalism, where television is decent and does not use pornographic figures to increase the rating, where they appeal to the intelligence and good morals of each person, not to low instincts and decadence.

A society where the virtuous woman who respects God's ways is the example and where the responsible, hard-working, and honourable man is the ultimate figure to follow.

Of course, there has always been evil; the problem is when bad people become the example to follow.

It is so important what examples a society has. A community where neither evil nor immorality nor uncleanness is the parameters to be followed, but where honour, decency, and respect for God and His ways are the north that traces the path to follow.

Where the grandparents have room for themselves, love, and attention, the holy and integral church has a voice and strength, being in charge of awakening the voice of the conscience and not extinguishing it.

Where good treatment is the norm, not the mistreatment. Where people who are alone and need someone to talk to are valued, and the family is loved and respected. Where no one feels alone but where everyone knows they are essential, listened to, and cared for.

A society where each individual can be fulfilled and where there are no standards for better or worse, but where the authenticity of each individual is valued.

A perfect society is not impossible; only hearts fearful of the law of God are needed. To respect authority again, not to challenge or destroy it, but to value those who teach us to be better parents, teachers, pastors, and even politicians who contribute to our progress.

Allegria was coming out of hell and dreamed of living in such a society, but despite her insistence, she still couldn't get out of the hell she was in; she couldn't get out of all that hell; it was like she was in her way to total liberation, but the hosts of evil were fighting to keep her inside.

She hated being on the frontier of hell, in a well. She already wanted to be in heaven.

Sometimes she couldn't go any further, so she would ask God to help her. As her relationship with Jesus increased, her intimacy with Him, the forces of evil gave way, and she set free herself as if she could come to the surface to leave hell behind; Jesus was the only one who could draw her out of that hell, from the well in which she was.

It was like a constant battle. The only true refuge she had was Jesus, her firm rock, who could take her out of that miry mud where her soul was.

When the battle was raging, Allegria ran to hide in privacy and spent her time reading the Holy Bible until she fell asleep; it was the only way she could find peace.

Allegria read Psalms repeatedly, meditated and thought about these truths.

The only one who could get her out of that hell was Jesus, so all she could do was meditate over and over again on that truth; as she thought about these truths, she began to believe them, assimilated them, and knew she could get out of that hell, she knew that someday she would get out of that hell.

Jesus brought her peace, joy, faith, and hope. She knew that only Jesus would change her story, that he would change her luck, and that she needed just to keep walking and trusting in God.

She was safe with Jesus, but getting out of hell was a process, and that process was going on in the "pilgrimage to freedom".

Coming out of hell is a process because when your soul has been living in so much darkness, you must re-learn many things and when your mind changes, your reality will change. That was the process Allegria was going through. It was difficult, but one must face a battle to be truly free.

Hell had her trapped; in other words, it was not that her soul had belonged to hell, but that there were things that stopped her from having that great life in the dreamed promised land.

However, Allegria was determined and objective, so she had decided to get out of hell, to fight what she had to fight but to get out of where she had to.

So strong was her desire to get out of that hellish place, and sometimes she seemed to be chased by the shadows as if they were telling her that she could not, that she could never get out of that place, that it was impossible, when in fact it was not, there was a battle to fight. Still, it was not impossible to get out from where she was.

Allegria ran to get out of the surface of that hell; the suffering was infinite, and it seemed like she would never be able to be completely free, to get out of the well where she was, even though she was no longer in the centre of hell. Still, it was difficult for her to leave the surface of suffering. It was like an immense and eternal great well, the landscape her soul had surrounded. She still was in that well.

It was a constant, oppressive, and exhausting battle.

Every day Allegria needed to pray and read the Bible to have the strength to continue. It was the only time she could find true peace.

The problem seemed to repeat itself. It was like one has been longing to get out of some hardship or get rid of something awkward in life, and that something seems endless. It was like living on a solid desire to escape some situation. That was the feeling that Allegria felt, and she was exhausted, but at the same time, she was determined to set herself free; it would change her luck, and she would finally be free and rejoice in true everlasting freedom.

The good news is that gradually, as she was heading to the exit each day, she was comforted by Jesus's visit, which strengthened her and encouraged her to keep fighting.

One day in particular, Allegria was not in the best shape; although she was still walking to escape that hell, the shadows reminded her of Costantino.

They were the shadows whispering that she was destined for a life of pain and curse, which is why she could never escape that hell. These shadows began to take hold; she tried to keep them away by slapping the air and covering her ears; it was like a constant torture from which Allegria only wanted to escape.

Allegria was beginning to weaken; she sometimes believed that she could not go on any longer and that the wind would blow her away. In her weakest moment, Costantino's exact figure appears as if he wants to seduce her, although, in reality, he only wants to play with her feelings to plunge her deeper into ruin and despair.

Allegria was so hungry, thirsty, and cold. She was devoid of hope, exposed, and vulnerable. It had been days since she had seen Jesus. No matter how hard she looked for him, her resistance was being tested.

Costantino appears in that moment of greatest weakness because evil will never manifest when you are strong; evil will display when you are weak in your most challenging affliction. Allegria was fighting a battle between life and death, but what was getting worse, she no longer had the strength. She started to feel spiritless.

The figure of Costantino began to recite beautiful words, words of love, like "I miss you, I need you, please don't leave me, don't walk away from me", and other sweet phrases. Costantino didn't love Allegria; he was provoking her to destroy her.

Allegria felt so hungry, dry, lonely, and finished; that was when Costantino's soul presented itself to her, offering her supposed joy, love, companionship, goodness, and fulfilment.

The figure of Costantino insisted, "Come on, take my hand, take my heart; you can't do it alone; it seems that Jesus stopped helping you; come on, take my hand, and everything will be fine".

That night Allegria fell asleep again, exhausted from crying so much, and she had a dream. In that dream, she looked like she was in a cell where the torment was endless; the whole past of pain, grief, and panic tortured her. She was petrified. The wrists on her hands were all sore, bleeding because the handcuffs were squeezing. She also had shackles on her feet. She could not move; she was captivated by fear. The oppression of the chains was so heavy that even she had trouble breathing. The depression overwhelmed her; she thought she'd never escape it.

Suddenly the door opens, the key is not locked, and Jesus appears, looking at her with such love and tenderness as a father would pamper his two-year-old daughter. He tells her that she is free, that she is entirely free, and that she is no longer enslaved. At that moment, the handcuffs and the shackles broke. Allegria smiled and burst into tears with happiness. She embraced Jesus and left the cell, rejoicing in her freedom.

Once out of the cell, she sees heaven wide open. A prince was waiting for her. This prince took her by the right hand and held her so that she would no longer fall into hell but would take the impulse to go upwards to heaven. She hears the prince say, "I'll never let you fall, come on, you can make it".

As she walks towards heaven, she sees, in the distance, down into hell and all the cursed figures used to seduce people to walk in a life of doom. She saw many people devoted to evil, serving the beast and his purposes, but she understood that she had the opportunity to be free.

That's when she woke up from her dream and realized she couldn't give up. When she turned her back to Costantino, he was still there, and Allegria looked him in the eye with total determination and said, "You've always promised a lot but never kept your promise. Why should it be different now if you've only lied? You've always lied".

The figure of Costantino insists, "Come on, this time everything will be different, this time I will change, this time everything will be better, I promise you heaven, I promise you the best, I will take you to heaven, no more pain, no more abandonment, no more loneliness, just you and me, both of us embraced in happiness forever".

Allegria sighed; she was so exhausted and took Costantino's hand at her weakest moment, but it was because she had something on her mind. She had seen heaven, which strengthened her inwardly, although she was still frail.

The figure of Costantino begins to say, "Well, I have won; now I possess your soul, I am its owner, and I will be able to do with it whatever I want because, after all, I don't want you to go to heaven and leave this hell forever". The shadow was using the figure of Costantino trying to hold her back. That was how the hell tried the hardest counterattack.

There is everyday suffering, like when a loved one dies, when a job is lost or when one is sick. Still, there is demonic suffering, that is, when the soul is tortured by bad decisions, by bad relationships, like the Kafkaesque feeling, when one suffers so much for so little, and that was the kind of suffering that Allegria suffered and had to be strong and get away from all that evil at once.

Allegria took Costantino's hand and looked him in the eye; she, who was very perceptive, saw in Costantino's eyes only hatred her.

Allegria understands that Costantino doesn't love her, that he has never loved her and that he wants to destroy her. Costantino thought he could fool Allegria once again, even smilingly seeming to enjoy his victory, as she let go of the hand of the figure of Costantino, having a strength she had never had before, a supernatural power, a conviction and fortitude seized her body and says to the formation of Costantino: "Let go of me, let go of me right now, I never belonged to you, and I never will belong to you, you can never have my soul! Leave my life right now; I will resist, Jesus will come to save me, but I will never again give in by descending into the infernal depths because only evil can be expected from the wicked one, and that is you, an evil one, who hides with the appearance of love and goodness when in reality you do not truly love anyone, you only love your pleasures and yourself, you mock all of us, all the others who try to go ahead and do good, I do not believe you anymore; you and your lies are leaving my life right now, and I don't care if I die here, I'd rather die here fighting for a better life than believing you again, you and your whole legion of destruction will disappear from my life. Costantino, you never loved me and you only wanted to destroy me".

The figure of Costantino reacts and realizes that he will no longer be able to deceive Allegria and says, "I see, you are better than me; even though I have done you a lot of harm, you have always done me good. But if someone can kill an enemy, do not let him go alive; that is me, your enemy. So I ask God to reward you with many good things for how well you have always treated me. I know you will get to heaven, to that dreamland you long to live in".

She rejoices with a mixture of feelings, between compassion and sorrow, pain and anger, and replies to him: "I wish you all the happiness in the world; although the path you've chosen will not make you happy, I still wish you to be pleased, and though I ever talk about you, I will remember you with compassion, now leave me because our time is over and I am determined to go to heaven, to live my dreamland, and dwell in it".

The figure of Costantino immediately disappears as Jesus appears. Allegria had passed the test, and the consolation of Jesus filled the heart of Allegria, who had been promoted and was already a few steps away from coming entirely out of that hell forever.

Allegria smiled again; Jesus was with her, and nothing could go wrong. "What, then, shall we say in response to these things? If God is for us, who can be against us?" (Romans 8:31).

Nothing and no one could end Allegria's life because God was with her; Jesus fought her battles and gave her victory so that she could be calm and safe even in her escape from that hell.

Allegria was determined to get out of that hell. God supports our determination. It's amazing what we accomplish when we're determined. It's like you have an inner strength you didn't think you had, all your energy is focused on the goal, and you start to organize yourself better, having a productive life. No matter how bad your life has been, it can change for the better. And that is what Allegria was looking for, a change. May everything in your life change for the better, leave all that evil behind and live a blessed present, heaven.

***

Sometimes Allegria wondered why so many people had chosen hell as if they were used to that hell instead of becoming better people. They prefer to become the worst version of themselves, something that gradually manifested itself.

The answer to this question is simple: when we do not obey God's principles, we become savage people. When we do not obey His laws, we are deteriorating and self-destructing in such a way that instead of becoming a gentleman or a lady, the opposite becomes out; a monster, someone crooked, degenerate, disobedient, sinful, banal, depressed and no apparent reason for which to live life.

When Esau sold his blessing to Jacob for a plate of lentils, time passed, and Jacob received the gift; Esau received nothing, generating a bid among them, so Esau became a savage, but Jacob became the father of a nation.

The point is that Esau despised God's blessing, and for God to bless us, there are parameters to follow; Jacob appreciated God's gift and followed those parameters, so he ended up receiving God's gift.

***

Allegria wanted to go out of hell, and she had to overcome another barrier: formalism. This happens when your soul and heart are already one foot out of place, but you must go through the gates of formality.

The impossibility had already been overcome because Jesus had already granted that victory to Allegria, which she had already achieved in the spiritual world; now, in her material world, she had to overcome the barriers of formalism.

Those walls sometimes spoke and seemed to tell Allegria that she couldn't make it, that she couldn't get out of the hell she was in, that formalism would never let her do it and that she would prepare to live an eternity in that damn hell because the circumstances were still hellish.

We should tell Allegria that God opens doors in another place when everyone rejects us. Those doors are even better because formalism may leave her and tell her that she doesn't have the size to live in a heaven of realities. Still, circumstances lie, and she had to learn to not believe whatever circumstances could say because the one who lived inside her was greater than the one who lived in the world.

The world for the worldly people was incredibly fantastic; the world smiled at Costantino; he had everything, fame, money, fortune, and power, and he was immensely popular; of course, he would go to hell, and his life was in hell, but everything seemed to smile at him. At the same time, everything was difficult for Allegria, she had no money, she had been left with nothing, her life had been destroyed, and she had to rebuild it from scratch; she was not popular, but heaven was smiling on her, and her life had begun to be ordered from the roots.

There is a reason why faith is not logical; sometimes, the essential, which is the soul, cannot be valued with the eyes. God sees hearts and not circumstances.

Allegria wanted to escape and go to that heaven where she had seen a prince. A prince she knew was waiting for her.

Hell opens immensely the doors to those who are lost because it knows that it will charge them with their soul. Hell always gives gifts or comforts to those who serve it.

***

Allegria rejoiced to strengthen her faith and decided to cover her ears and listen only to the truth of God; all day long, she read the Holy Bible, repeated His promises, and kept sober to keep her sanity in such hell. It was a constant battle between life and death; every day mattered, every second counted, and every millisecond of her life was at stake.

Allegria was a warrior and had learned to resist; she would not let herself be defeated in battle. She was trained to fight, not to give up, and she was there to win. She repeated in her mind, "I'm going to get out of this; God is going to help me, and I'm going to win if God is with me; who is against me?" Allegria knew a sweet victory awaited her.

Allegria was a brilliant and beautiful woman. She was more intelligent than attractive; her intelligence made her attractive, and everything she was going through helped her develop her character. Having a character trained in discipline and perseverance is a quality for true beauty; it is an attribute to be a winner, and Allegria wanted to be a winner.

She knew she needed to endure the formal process to escape that hell. She was determined to leave behind hell forever.

She had to be able to go through that stage, and that stage demanded patience and intelligence. Intelligence to do the right thing and patience to endure the process while she waits.

Intelligence is accompanied by wisdom. Wisdom is doing the right thing in life with your choices, and patience is how we react while waiting. We need to develop character while waiting.

Suddenly impatience arose with fury, with force capable of devouring her, but she resisted. She knew she had to be patient because she was only hours away from getting out of hell. The only thing she could do was endure; her release was on its way. She was determined not to give in. She wouldn't give up. She would win. She wouldn't go back. She would come out of that hell, from all that damned hell and go on to live the blessing, that blessing of a dreamed earth and open heaven.

Sometimes Allegria was so exhausted and fell asleep waiting for her total liberation, to come out of the surface of hell to live a heavenly reality.

Sometimes while she slept, she dreamed that heaven was opening for her and that a beautiful young man, a prince, was waiting for her, that this man was good and feared God. Everything in that heavenly place was full of light, and that young man held her hand and helped her out of the hell she was living in.

When she woke up the next day, having had a good rest, she had renewed strength and was even happy because she longed for this dream to come true in the depths of her heart.

***

Sometimes the memories of so many failures, darkness, and shadows whispered to her that she would fail or be unable to achieve it. However, she opened her Bible and reread it every time King David defeated his enemies and filled himself with faith; so she became strong.

Leading by impatience, one can make many mistakes. That's when you must be attentive and careful to do the right thing and keep doing the right thing until you get out of hell for good.

Allegria knew this, so she resisted. She resisted with all her strength; she knew she had to be strong, and this was the time to win.

Impatience was plagued with evil: foolishness, coarseness, stubbornness, and everything that does not contribute to a person's life. Impatience presented itself as a strong man who wanted to devour her. This strong man stood before her and insulted her. He embarrassed and humiliated her as if to say, "Do you think you'll hold out? Won't you give up? Do you think you can still resist?"

Allegria prayed for help from the Holy Spirit and implored: "Father, give me strength to resist, that I may not retaliate by damaging what I should not. I pray that you will come to punish my enemies like you will punish the strong forces who wanted to stop me in hell".

One must be calm and know how to wait when coming out of hell. Many people are on a waiting list to go down to hell because their time is running out here on earth, and it is another thing to wait to get out of hell and never go back to that hell again.

Many people are on a waiting list for a transplant, for an operation, for a storm to end, for an earthquake to cease... and others are waiting to get out of the hell that their lives have been transformed into and never return to it.

That's what Allegria was hoping for to get out of hell, so she had to learn to be patient, wait, be thankful to God and resist, resist because her waiting was worth it.

She expected to go out. She expected to be completely free, not to descend. Others expect the worst; she was waiting for the best.

Think of all that she had already endured and resisted; it was a matter of a little more, and she would be free forever.

Some people have been waiting to go to prison, and Allegria waited to get out of jail, so it was worth the wait.

The blessed day has come at last… heaven opens up, and she begins to walk the last steps to leave hell behind once and for all.

Allegria received the news: "She would be set free". Her pass was sealed with the blood of Christ, and she would be accessible in a matter of hours.

***

Allegria was intelligent and wise, she only fought when God sent her, so she was sure that God would make all her descendants reign and influence the earth. Because she neither now nor ever gave up on doing the wrong thing.

If someone tried to persecute her and wanted to destroy her, God would take care of her, and she would be safe. For those who want to destroy her soul, God will throw them away, just like a stone is thrown with a slingshot.

Allegria will be the leader who emerged from hell and went out to tell the tale, for God was fulfilling all the promises He had made to her. She'd walk out, walk out free, walk out now… in a few more steps. The door was already open; she'd walk free.

When that happens, she won't feel guilty for hurting people, and she would not take revenge because she did everything she could to save them and take them with her, but they loved the shadows more than light, and it was time for her to go free, to go free forever.

Allegria knew it was a matter of seconds, seconds more, and she would be free. So while those seconds were coming, because the heaven was already open for Allegria, she prayed: "Blessed be the God of Israel, who remembered me, and blessed be the Holy Spirit who gave me the intelligence and wisdom so that I would not take revenge and decide to act on my own, but who made me resist and now I am seconds away from living my complete freedom, blessed be God, who punished evil and set me free! He took revenge for the evil they did to me. Hallelujah!".

Allegria was on her way to freedom; the order had been given; a few more steps, and she would leave for good, never to return to that hell again. However, time was trying to stop her; therefore, she would have to know how to proceed faster than time. The environment was like it wanted to numb her.

Time stood before her like a giant monster that began to spit at her and curse her, "You're not coming out, you ain't' coming this time, it's too late, it can't be done, you're not going to make it".

Time throws flames of fire and attacks her with a sword; its way of proceeding is numbness and lethargy, as if one surrendered to the situation and did nothing contrary as if one accepted the position and did not fight against it. It was crazy.

Allegria fought to stay awake and not fall asleep. How did she manage to do so? She prayed, praised God, fasted, read the Holy Bible and repeated verses.

In this way, Allegria stayed awake and at a sufficient pace to overcome the lethargy that seemed to want to flood her in the final stretch.

Allegria was beating time. The Holy Spirit himself comforted her, and she seemed to take power from nowhere and continue to resist, to endure, to overcome time. Sometimes the monster of time seemed so big that it was as if this was such impossible to defeat it that she should give in, but at the moment of most extraordinary fragility, she received strength from heaven.

Allegria was brave; she did not give up, and she knew she would win because God was on her side; that was the only great secret; God was on her side, not against her, on her side; this made her unstoppable and invincible. As Psalm 46:7 says, "The LORD Almighty is with us".

Make sure you are always in God's plans because those plans work and are great, your projects end up being your biggest nightmare, but God's plans start, work, light up, and even walk alone without you having to push them.

God's plans flow into your life, and you learn to sail with them, not the other way around. While your will is crude, absurd, and brutal, God's plans are sweet, praiseworthy, honourable, and worthy.

Costantino had been such a good man, apparently, he had no flaws, but as appearances deceive, he was the worst man.

Allegria was imperfect; her faults were visible to the naked eye, but her heart was pleasing God, which is where true beauty lies.

***

Allegria kept praying and asking God for help, chanting aloud different verses to encourage herself as she waited for the last few seconds.

She read and meditated in Psalm 144, "Part your heavens, LORD, and come down; touch the mountains, so that they smoke. Send forth lightning and scatter the enemy; shoot your arrows and rout them. Reach down your hand from on high; deliver me and rescue me from the mighty waters, from the hands of foreigners whose mouths are full of lies, whose right hands are deceitful. I will sing a new song to you, my God; o the ten-stringed lyre, I will make music to you, to the One who gives victory to Kings, who delivers his servant David".

Allegria was begging for mercy and holiness; she needed to get out of that situation, out of the company of bad people, and start a new life again.

When you humiliate yourself before God, He hears and answers you because God has compassion on those who fear Him, in other words, those who respect Him.

Allegria, when she waited for her release, knew that she did not live a great love, that everything was a lie, a deception, but no more. Allegria's heart did not love Costantino anymore, she felt nothing for him anymore, nothing but compassion and sorrow. Allegria's heart no longer felt any love for him, nothing remained.

All Allegria wanted was to get out of hell.

Allegria had overcome all the games of hunger, endured all the embarrassment, and survived all the misfortunes; now, she wanted to be free.

Allegria's heart no longer waited for Costantino to return and be saved; she only wanted to never return to that state where he had left her.

***

She was fulfilling the last stage of hellish formalism, but the decree had already been given; she would be free. As she continued to wait for the remaining fractions of seconds, sometimes her heart would awaken and what a beautiful feeling she had when she knew that she no longer expected anything from Costantino, that she no longer expected anything from him.

Her heart had been free, and one day, the day she wasn't even aware of, Allegria came out of hell. She'll never forget it was April 19, 1996. God made it with paper in hand. She received the decree from God, and her soul was completely free.

Allegria wept with happiness and kissed the paper; the decree God had signed was already coming out of hell, and she saw before her eyes how the hell had the floodgates of terror; behind it, she left the cries of terror and anguish. She left the tortures of the soul behind. She was free. She was completely free and knew she'd never return to that damn place again.

She had defeated hell, the darkness, formalism, and impossibility. She left behind everything that had tormented her.

She was taking steps to leave behind her most significant and profound agony. She was leaving that cursed land behind forever.

By April 20, the floodgates roared. She took her first step in the land of freedom; she was on her way to living a heavenly reality.

Glory to God; he did it! Allegria was crying of happiness; she could not believe she was so pleased; she had not remembered being so happy in so many years.

Hallelujah! Because freedom has come at last, God hears our prayers, and our heart matters to Him.

God had decided to take revenge on the enemies of Allegria; He had decided to take revenge on the enemies of the cross; He had agreed to give victory to Allegria by humiliating once and for all the enemies of the cross, those who would rather be friends of the whole damn system of the world than be friends of God.

The victorious God was present, defending Allegria and destroying her enemies. As Nahum 1.2 says, "The Lord is jealous and avenging God; the Lord takes vengeance and is filled with wrath. The Lord takes vengeance on his foes and vents his wrath against his enemies".

Allegria proved that it was true what Psalms 92:9 says: "For surely your enemies, Lord, surely your enemies will perish; all evildoers will be scattered".

Allegria saw that the doers of iniquity went down to perish forever. Still, God had mercy on those who repented their wickedness and left behind their evil ways.

God took revenge on evil by giving total and complete freedom to the life of Allegria. Allegria had defeated her enemies.

Allegria raised her hands in praise of God; she wept with joy… she was immensely grateful to God for his mercy, for having rescued her from that hell.

***

Allegria could not understand so much love from God for her life. She was impressed and deeply grateful. As Peter Furler sang: "You hold the weight of the world. Still, I don't slip through your hands;

your love is bigger than just an ocean built by man, I fall again and again, but you whisper, 'You're still mine' You feel the pain of the world, but you never push mine aside. And you reach for me with a love that quiets all my fears, and you reach for me as a father wipes away the tears; so many people in this world, but I hear you calling out my name. You reach for me; now, I will never be the same. You know all my fears. Nothing your eyes can't see; when I tried to give up, Lord, you never gave up on me. I give you all my hopes and dreams; I lay them down. You're the one truth I have found in all the places I've looked".

The day Allegria came out of hell, she had a vision. She saw herself as a little girl, dressed in white and running to the arms of the Heavenly Father, and he embraced and kissed her, held her in his arms and comforted her. She was already free and would not return to slavery; she was out of hell.

God is always good, and He hears our prayers and answers them. Without a doubt, God always replies to our prayers.

Allegria coming out of hell was an answer to her prayer.

Why did Allegria come out of hell? Because God Himself was her refuge and protection, as Psalms 91:9 says, "If you say, 'The Lord is my refuge', and you make the Most High your dwelling".

Allegria didn't perish in the flames of hell. God wanted to rescue her because God understands hearts and knows when our supplication is sincere and when we repent and want to order our lives.

God heard Allegria's cry and set her free.

Chapter 10
**"If thou follow thy star, thou canst not fail of glorious heaven".
Dante Alighieri**

It was already 1999. So far this decade, many things have happened. One of them was the Internet boom. The Internet was used with the telephone line making a lot of noise. The first wireless phones appeared. Many good things were happening in that beautiful decade.

Let's recap, what did we experience in the 1990s? It was the decade of Clinton, Pablo Escobar, Mandela, Kurt Urbain, and Power Rangers. We were shaken by the deaths of Princess Diana and Mother Teresa of Calcutta, and perhaps the most notorious case was the murder for which O.J. Simpson was incriminated, until now, he has not convinced us of his acquittal.

Another important figure was the person of Saddam Hussein and the Persian Gulf War. Another unfortunate confrontation was in the Balkans.

It was a time of good World Cups like Italy 90, the USA 94, and France 98.

Great films like "Clueless" and "The Bodyguard" appeared with the beautiful voice of Withney Houston, who delighted us with the song "I Will Always Love You". The movie "You Got a Mail" was presented, which introduced us to a new way of finding love, something unthinkable in the 1980s. Then the cinema exploded with the absolute box-office record "Titanic" with her iconic song "My Heart Will Go On" by Céline Dion.

It was the decade of portable games, cassettes, and video cassettes. The decade that Michael Jackson and Madonna were crowned as the king and queen of pop music. Britney Spears, Christina Aguilera, and Back Street Boys were sounding a lot everywhere, and NSYNC appeared with their classic "Bye, bye, bye" and the hit that broke all records and made all cultures dance emerged: "Macarena!".

The following words give us an idea of what we experienced in the 90s: Internet Explorer. Steve Jobs. MTV. Anorexia. U2. Nintendo. Wild liberalism. The cloned sheep. Pete Sampras. Andre Agassi.

Life is beautiful. Thank you so much. My legs were cut off. Fall off the Berlin Wall. Clinton and Monica Lewinsky scandal.

And, of course, the phrase: "The end of the world will happen in 2000!"

Life had become beautiful again for Allegria, and she enjoyed herself daily.

Allegria woke up to go to work with the sound of the church bells and was as happy as she had ever been! Nothing spectacular happened in her daily life; she was only delighted, enjoying her relationship with God, herself and Aosta.

Aosta was one big family. She'd wake up, make hot coffee, and go to work at the store. The usual clothing store had a beautiful family clientele. They all knew each other and treated each other with great affection. They were all part of everyone.

Allegria sometimes went to lunch at a client's house. Many of her clients were older women, so the deal was from a nonna to a granddaughter.

Allegria loved her new life; she felt like she was born again and that God was giving her a unique chance to do everything right, even better than before.

This new life was dignified, decent, and disciplined without pain; therefore, she rejoiced in a life full of peace.

She had hit rock bottom, had already gone through all the stages of pain, and had suffered all kinds of deprivations and needs, but now she was waking up to life and thanking God for every day she had to live. She had lost everything, but now she had everything. She had God, and she had peace. What else could she ask for? It took her time to get to that place of peace, but now she enjoyed it to the fullest; now she was happy, pleased from within.

Allegria had learned to love the good, the good habits, the home, the small delights of life: riding a bicycle, having a coffee, holding the hand of the nonna, smiling at the mamma, and mangiare la pasta al pesto.

Now she knew how to enjoy her parents, with whom she had a healthy and solid relationship. It's funny Allegria's parents never liked Costantino, and time shows that her parents were correct. There is a reason why we should always listen to parents' advice. Sometimes, parents can see beyond what we see and read intentions that we, as young, do not realise.

She learned to enjoy Sundays with her family, where all the uncles, cousins and nephews gathered, and she was so happy!

Allegria's life was surrounded by goodness and virtue. Her life has been transformed into a life of good.

Sometimes, she was afraid that hell would threaten to return, but she meditated on Psalm 40:17, which says, "But as for me, I am poor and needy; may the Lord think of me. You are my help and my deliver; you are my God, do not delay". Her heart was regaining strength. She knew the God who delivered her would not let her fall off the cliff again.

Allegria understood that not to return to hell. She had to do the right thing repeatedly until it became part of her way of being, part of her mind and will. At that moment, she began to live a heavenly reality. She needed to do the right thing, be brave, and never give up. Making sacrifices to endure the sufferings to reach the goal of living a heavenly reality, and God helps if she does not give up; if she is determined, God helps.

Allegria was going through the whole detoxification process, and she loved it; she was happy to cleanse her soul, to remove from inside everything that had damaged her for so long.

Throughout this healing process, Allegria sometimes went to Aosta's public library or up the mountain to ski. She loved warming herself in winter, drinking coffee, and then skiing at the Alpine peaks. Allegria had become an outstanding sportswoman. In the summer, she was preparing for athletics. Allegria was a good runner; she had a good physical constitution, which helped her in any sport. In winter, she went to ski, in summer, she went to run.

***

Allegria, as she went to church every Sunday and had beautiful experiences throughout that period, saw again how beautiful life was. While riding the bike, she could see the beautiful scenery surrounding the city of Aosta. The town was lively, seeing the mothers with their children, watching students leaving school, and young people sharing a meal and laughing. Wow! A new awakening had come into her life. She was grateful to be born again.

Italy is significant, but now it's like Allegria was rediscovering it. She enjoyed every little detail of her nation.

She rejoiced every Sunday when she attended the services in the church and listened to the exposition of the Bible; her soul was healed. Allegria had changed and as sang Il volo "L'amore si muove, ti porta lontano se vuoi, ti prende per mano senza dirti dove andrai, l'amore si muove, e non fa rumore lo sai, é un vento gentile che non ti abbandona mai".

Yes, Allegria was ready to experience love again, true love… everything had changed, and she was ready to go away from everything that had hurt her. She was prepared to let herself be carried out by true love… because everything had changed and moved, and now her heart was different; it was better. There was nothing left of the false love between her and Costantino. Allegria was now mature enough to experience true love, an everlasting love.

She was dressing up in love because her soul was healing. She had learned the importance of having a forgiving heart; she had no grudge, and she had forgiven all the past because she understood that if she wanted to be happy, she must forgive everyone who hurt her and not hold a single grudge.

Bless those people and forget the damage they have done because, in the end, it is God who fixes injustice. If she wants God's forgiveness, she must learn to develop forgiveness for all who hurt her. As the letter to the Colossians says: "And over all these virtues put on love, which binds them all together in perfect unity".

Only true forgiveness sets our souls free.

She was free; she knew how to forgive and forget. In her memory, she kept only good stories worth telling. She did not control all the filthy things; she only treasured good memories… all the memories of her beloved native land: "Aosta".

***

Allegria's life has become meaningful again. She began to help the "Sisters of Charity" in the church. Allegria on Monday, Wednesday and Friday. They visited needy families, provided them with food and clothing, and wrote about who needed to see a doctor.

She was going to collaborate on the social welfare service and see people in need three days a week.

Since Allegria had taken pedagogy classes at university, she helped the children with their homework; she was patient with the children who needed the most attention. In wintertime, Allegria would light the fireplace and stay in the church dining room, helping the children.

Winter was harsh, intense, and heavy. There was so much snow and many shortages, but she did not give up and continued to do her work every day whenever they needed her to help.

Allegria made herself loved by all those low-income families, and the Sisters of Charity loved her. Allegria was as happy as she had ever thought she could be because we are so glad when we give. The key to happiness is true generosity. When you're not self-centred and serve others, serve the most needed ones and exercise love together with compassion and mercy.

Allegria in Aosta was very self-fulfilled. She had learned to be happy with whatever circumstances came her way. She had made new friends, more friends, while perhaps losing some contact with her old friends, but that did not affect her so much because now she was a friend of justice, peace, and joy. In other words, she didn't need any specific people to be happy with; she was delighted to enjoy the company of anyone who showed up at work, at university, or in the underprivileged neighbourhood she attended. She was pleased with the sisters of faith. It was a new world, but that world was whole, and she was complete, as she had never been.

In the deprived neighbourhood, she learned a lot; she knew that despite not having so much, there were substantial homes, noble families, parents who worked to give the best to their children, and obedient children who sacrificed themselves studying because they wanted a better future.

Allegria understood in all that time that the ultimate goal was not to reach her objective because you can get the goals alone and still be alone; instead, the goal was to achieve the objectives with people, to fulfil her plans with loving people, to help her neighbour to achieve it because if she allows someone else performs it, God will make her reach the goal too. After all, the key is not to attain self-set targets but rather to share and serve.

Allegria's heart was changing. She had become a better person with this whole process. Allegria understood that God would reward each one according to his justice and his truth and that it was worthless to grieve for the evil received since what you sow comes to reap, God gives pay and retribution.

If you receive sin, God will provide you with good because God is the only one who can give you beauty in exchange for all the ashes you have experienced.

She understood that mercy makes us happy. Allegria had learned this from seeing the "Sisters of Charity" testimony. It was amazing to see how these nuns served with so much love and selflessness, as they generously gave to others and sought all their good. This impacted her. Seeing such an example, she agreed that she would dedicate herself to holiness, a godly and merciful life, and help her neighbour.

For this reason, she faithfully worked with the poor three days a week.

There was no competition, comparison, or need to be first; everyone was happy to give and share.

***

Sister Evangelina was the one Allegria most admired. Evangelina was modest, austere, dignified, and always had a smile on her face. She was dynamic and hardworking. She had no greed whatsoever.

Sometimes, sister Evangelina would take her bike late at night to take dinner to some families who had nothing to feed their children or themselves. She brought them the leftovers from the convent's dinner, and she did it from the very bottom of her heart because nobody forced her; it was not her job; she was moved by that true mercy and the desire that some needy people have something to eat with the cold that was lived in the Alps.

Sister Evangeline was extraordinary, entirely out of this world.

Allegria thinks about sister Evangelina and how this world has become so materialistic and only magnifies people who are after money, so she exclaims, "What's wrong with working and earning a decent monthly salary? What's wrong with working and striving, saving little by little and having dignity? What's wrong with having a good, honourable life that doesn't run after money?".

Because of how this world goes, it seems that it only matters to have money and to go after money, when in reality, the love of money only causes disorder and brings all kinds of sorrow. That was something that Allegria had learned, and that's why she only wanted to get together with decent, hardworking, and dynamic people; those people who didn't love money but loved souls, who loved people and valued them because every human being deserves to be respected and treated with dignity.

Sister Evangelina lived in this truth: "Keep your lives free from the love of money and be content with what you have, because God has said, "Never will I leave you; never will I forsake you". So we say with confidence, "The Lord is my helper; I will not be afraid. What can mere mortals do to me?" (Hebrews 13:5 and 6). She was a woman without deception, transparent, and sincere.

Allegria had seen so much deception in people who were on their way to hell, especially in the heresy part, where they were: "having a form of godliness but denying its power. Have nothing to do with such people" (2 Timothy 3:5), or as God speaks today would say in another version: "will appear to be very spiritual, but by their deeds will deny the true power of a spiritual life. Don't have anything to do with that kind of people", which is why she didn't want to be with that kind of people anymore. All she had suffered had served her to differentiate the truth from the false.

Allegria was fed up with appearances and falsehoods; she wanted to see a genuine faith, an authentic faith, and that is what she saw in sister Evangelina, which is why she admired her so much.

Maybe Allegria had been so deceived that she couldn't stand it anymore; she wanted to be sincere, honest, and transparent in her life because she understood that it's never too late to do it well in life, that you can be wrong many times; still, if you sincerely and wholeheartedly repent, you get to have new opportunities and no matter how much trouble you are in, God has enough love to help you solve all your problems.

She understood that she could learn again, that she could do well, and that with patience and love, she would reach her destination. If you do the right thing over and over again, sooner or later, victory comes, and good things happen. Because goodness always overcomes evil.

Allegria had decided to do the right thing; she had abandoned all evil and only wanted to do the right thing, make the right choice, do what's right with integrity, and straighten out all her paths, and this is what she was doing. She was cleaning up her life, fixing all her problems with someone like Costantino. At times, it was challenging to be alone and resolve so many dilemmas to heal the heart, but she needed to go through this healing time.

As she healed, she experienced how beautiful life was and was grateful to God for every little detail she could live each day. Every morning, the mercies of God on her life were new, and she could see God's love every day.

Allegria had put these verses in Psalms 19:10 and 11 as the headline; "They are more precious than gold than much pure gold; they are sweeter than honey from the honeycomb. By then, your servant is warned; in keeping them, there is great reward". Allegria had cleansed her heart; she wanted only the goodness of God and only the honourable things. She had definitively abandoned all that was crooked; she had abandoned Costantino and any remote idea of being with him.

Allegria's family was pleased to see such good changes in her; this new Allegria was so different, beautiful from the inside, and comfortable.

***

Allegria sometimes dreamed of a prince when she went to bed; he was a handsome, gorgeous young man, full of calm and light. This young man was dressed in royal robes and was in heaven, in a heavenly reality and reached out to Allegria as if to rescue her.

She has had this dream over and over again. When she woke up, she remembered the dream, and such a good and tender man gave her hope… hope that one day she would find such a man and she could live in true love.

One day, in the middle of winter, Allegria decided to go with sister Evangelina to a family in the mountains of the Alps to take them food. They were migrants who had problems with their papers and could not work until their document problems were resolved. Walking in the middle of the forest with so much snow was difficult, but sister Evangelina faithfully fulfilled her vocation there.

Allegria thought aloud, "It is so cold, and we are in the middle of the mountains. Imagine what it will be like in the Scandinavian countries, like Denmark, which has no mountains". Sister Evangelina sighed and said, "Thank you, daughter, for that comment! I had forgotten that we received a letter from the Lutheran Mission of the Danish People's Church; they will discuss some agreements and new programs for organising the church's social welfare. Here, we only speak Italian, and you are doing very well with English; I thought that you could go on our representation and bring us all the information we need to continue learning because I want someone to go there, learn and teach us. You are the chosen one".

Allegria smiled happily and said, "Do you mean I'll go to replace you!? Wow, what a joy; I always wanted to know about Denmark; it's a beautiful country, the land of Hans Christian Andersen, the land of fairy tales. Of course, dear sister, I will go and learn everything I can learn to innovate in this work of social help". Sister Evangelina replies, "I'm glad, my daughter, that God accompanies you; you have been of great help; thank you for all the work you've done to help us with our work. Now, let's continue walking because the Saadi family await for us".

Allegria and sister Evangelina put on so many clothes because of the harsh winter that it was hard for them to walk. So strong winds and so much snow that it was scary. It's just that winter in the Alps. Everything is foreseen in God's will, and God had a beautiful plan that would happen on this journey. Excellent and beautiful blessings were awaiting Allegria in that new land.

***

The days she was continued to go by typically. Allegria now had to file some papers at the office because of her trip. So she used to go in the mornings to get permits and documents from the Municipality of Aosta and the church since she was representing the Sisters of Charity.

Winter had passed, and spring had come. Everything was starting to bloom. The beautiful flowers of Italy covered the landscape with their colour, the fragrance that the forest gave off and even the sound of the waters was heard because the snow was beginning to melt, to disappear.

Some families pruned the plants in the spring; others fertilized the vegetables in their garden… everything had begun to come alive; spring had arrived!

What a beautiful feeling Italy gives people in the mornings! When people go to the office, the shops that open their curtains, ready to start receiving people, the freshly baked bread, the smells, the flavours that come off, the bakeries that already have the bread ready and newly baked for all their customers... Oh, how beautiful Italy is! It's the perfect land.

Sometimes Allegria would go to lunch with the "Sisters of Charity" to save time. After lunch, they would continue to work on the papers. By then, Allegria had finished all her university studies and resigned from her job with the Ferrara family. Therefore, she was entirely dedicated to her work with the sisters in all social assistance matters.

***

It's so good Italian cuisine! Allegria loved it when the sisters prepared the ravioli alla carbonara. What a delight to the palate that dish was, but she secretly loved eating with the sisters since they were her great friends. Allegria was so happy with every minute she shared with them, with sister Evangelina, sister Amore, sister Fede, and sister Cristina.

Every country has its beauty, but Italy is the best country in the world "per mangiare".

Every day, sister Evangelina collects fresh bread from the bakery because the bread was donated to their charity, so always in the house of Charity, they have fresh bread and share it with the neediest ones.

In all that time, Allegria was preparing herself for the trip to Denmark.

One of the requirements for this trip to Denmark was that Allegria passed the medical test. She went to the hospital and had all the necessary tests done. Thank God she was in excellent physical condition; even the doctor told her that she had an athlete's heart because of the tremendous pulse rate with which her heart worked. Allegria smiled and said, "It's the work with the children; they make me stay in great shape".

That day, Allegria went to the bakery to buy some dumplings filled with Nutella; she had to celebrate in her own way, having received such excellent news.

***

Time had passed like a hurricane, and the day had come; Allegria had to take the train to go to Milan, as the plane was departing from that city, and fly to Copenhagen, Denmark.

She said goodbye to her parents and siblings. The congregation's sisters took her to the train station, but it seemed like a joke; the traffic was worse than ever, and Allegria feared missing the train, which would mean missing the flight.

Honking, screams, noise, and the typical gestures that Italians make as they join all the fingers of their right hand together as they say phrases like "Ma dai!" or "Ma va!" "Ma che vuole?" "Ma mi stai prendendo in giro?"

It's no wonder we all know that Italy is the most fun country in the world. You'll see a piccola opera wherever you go.

Thank God sister Evangelina accelerated with the car, CSI Miami style, and they could get to the station on time. Sister Evangelina was the complete combo. She had a heart like that of the disciple Peter, an emotional sensitivity like Mother Theresa, and drove the car like Ayrton Senna. She certainly knew how to achieve her goals.

As she said goodbye, Allegria hugged sister Evangelina and said, "Thank you for helping me out of the state I was in; thank you, I'm thrilled now!", "You're welcome, my dear, you're totally welcome!", replied sister Evangelina.

***

Allegria arrives at Milan station. She got on the train, and the adventure of a lifetime awaited her. The train station in Milan is impressive. Art. Sculpture. Without a doubt, Italy is the best country to tell the story of time.

The Stazione di Milano Centrale is one of the main railway stations in Europe. It's a railway terminal officially opened in 1931 to replace the old Central Station that had been built in (1864). This transit station could not handle the increase in passenger traffic caused by the opening of the Sempione Tunnel (1906). King Victor Emmanuel III of Italy laid the foundation stone for the new station on April 28, 1906, even before the project for the station had been defined. The final and official competition for its construction was won in 1912 by the architect Ulisse Stacchini. Due to the Italian economic crisis during the First World War, its construction advanced very slowly. The project, simple at first, was constantly changing and became more complex and majestic. This happened mainly when Benito Mussolini became Prime Minister, and he wanted the station to represent the power of the fascist regime.

Construction resumed in 1925, and Foreign Minister Galeazzo Ciano officially inaugurated the station on July 1, 1931.

Its facade is 200 metres wide, and its vault is 72 metres high, a record at the time. It has 24 platforms. Approximately 330,000 passengers use the station daily, totalling some 120 million annually.

The station does not have a defined architectural style but is a mixture of different types, including Art Nouveau and Art Deco.

It was a delight to be at this station, but Allegria could not stop to observe so much, as the minutes were running and she had to arrive at the airport on time.

She arrived at Milan's Malpensa airport and prepared to take the flight to Denmark. She was so excited. Her hands were sweating. She did not know why but felt this experience would change her life. And so it was.

When she arrived at the airport, a young man was waiting for her; he was part of the delegation of those who would give the social welfare conference.

Seeing each other was love at first sight as if they had known each other all their lives. Because everything is foreseen in God's will, and when Allegria saw him, she recognized the vision she had; he was the young man who was in heaven, the young man who was waiting for her.

The young man had a sign that read "Sisters of Charity". Allegria said to him, "Hi". He replied, "Hello, do you represent the Sisters of Charity?" She nodded and said she had come instead of them. He shakes her hand and says, "Buongiorno, I am Giovanni... Giovanni Medici". She smiles and answers: "I am Allegria... Allegria Disalvatore". A sparking love was born, the connection was total, and it was like they had been waiting for each other... forever.

He helps her with the suitcases and takes them to where the congress will be held. It was in a Lutheran church outside Copenhagen. The church was called Sct. Hans Kirke, who is short for Johannes. The days that followed were incredible.

They didn't separate for the entire conference. They shared every second and talked about everything. They were perfect together. That's right. They were perfect for each other. It's just like meeting someone with whom your soul fits perfectly. Well, that's how they felt.

Life in Denmark was a delight. To go to Congress, Giovanni and Allegria used bicycles. They ride a bike any distance, so fitting in that country was easy.

In Denmark, everything was in order and harmony. They have five meals a day. In the mornings, they wake up and have coffee with cereal for breakfast, then potatoes, pork, and bacon for lunch. The coffee schedule continues at around three or four in the afternoon. Dinner is at six o'clock, but it won't be all over with dinner; they return to have coffee with a few sponge cakes at ten o'clock in the evening. Danes love rye bread, coffee, bacon, sushi and pork. The Lutheran influence can be seen in every aspect of their formation as a society. That's the secret to why Denmark is such a great country. Denmark is a Dreamland.

They're experts at making delicious marzipan cakes. They have thousands of recipes.

There are no fears; it's a safe country, life is quiet, and everything happens in such a harmonious environment that makes life so welcoming. Without a doubt, all those days were, for Allegria, a caress to the soul.

There are big cities and small towns... and they all have charm. Allegria was happy with every second she spent in that land.

They say everything fits you when you're in the right place, and goodness spreads everywhere. That was Denmark for Allegria; everything smiled at her in that place, even love. Allegria didn't want the seminar to end. Giovanni wanted the same thing; he was so happy with Allegria's company. They were happy together, talking or in silence.

They smiled, held hands, walked, had their meals together, kept quiet, looked at each other… they smiled again. They looked like two teenagers in love.

On the penultimate day of the seminar, Allegria told Giovanni, "I don't want it to end; I don't want to leave". He took her hand and said, "I don't want you to leave either, but you will leave, and I will come and get you". They smiled, and both knew that was the beginning of their Dreamed-style romance that would last a lifetime.

When he says goodbye at the airport in Copenhagen, he says: "I'll see you soon; I'll come and get you". He caresses her face and kisses her on the lips. She responds to the kiss tenderly.

They loved each other and were happy, immensely happy! As delighted as they've ever been in their lives.

Giovanni was an outstanding young man. A great youngster. He was immensely handsome, like an angel. Blond, blue eyes, and a stunning physique. It looked like the David Michelangelo created. But he wasn't just beautiful on the outside; he was rich on the inside and full of virtues. He was patient, merciful, loyal, noble, loved righteousness, and trustworthy. He followed the law of God and had God in all his ways.

We cannot say that he was perfect because perfection only exists in God, but he was an almost ideal man because he walked with God daily.

He was like a gentleman, like those gentlemen you can take from fairy tales. So was Giovanni, one of the knights with a beautiful heart described by Hans Christian Andersen, the most significant Danish writer.

Giovanni sincerely loved Allegria, and she sincerely loved Giovanni. They were meant for each other.

Allegria was so excited about her return to Denmark that she seemed to dream of that happy world. Se had to take the train to

Torino to get to Aosta, but she missed the train because she had been thinking about Giovanni.

***

Giovanni Medici had Italian roots; his parents still lived and worked in Florence, the magnificent city of Florence.

When Allegria returned, she told the nuns and her family everything that had happened in Denmark. Everyone was happy for her. The letters between Giovanni and Allegria began to follow one after another, month after month. Then Giovanni goes to visit her in Aosta.

He found her collecting coats for underprivileged neighbourhoods. They look at each other, smile, and kiss. It was pure love.

Allegria had finished all her studies and only went to college while campaigning to collect coats for the immigrant neighbourhood. Giovanni liked to visit the university of Allegria in Aosta.

Allegria and Giovanni went on to enjoy their pure love... everything in a unique and new way. All that had been pain was now only joy in Allegria's life.

God had changed the ashes of Allegria's life into deep joy.

Giovanni was an actual prince who knew how to act like one. He had the bearing of a prince and the conduct of a prince. When you have such a good man by your side, who loves you, respects you and treats you so well every day of your life, what more can you ask for in love?

He had come to spend his holidays with her, and Allegria lived love over again but in a healing way. They walked together through the streets of Aosta, they enjoyed together through the Roman ruins, the Roman restaurant, the walls of Augustus Caesar, the restaurants on the Alps, listening again to the songs of love in Italian, seeing young people preparing for the Olympics... everything was back to life, but in a unique way, memorable and full of joy and delight.

Now she was in a healthy relationship and was pleased.

***

During the week, they helped the Sisters of Charity, helping the children of Don Bosco's school. Everything expanded air of goodness and kindness. Sometimes on Friday nights, they went to the music conservatory to listen to the symphonies of Händel and Bach.

On one of these visits to the conservatory, they passed by a tree that was more than 1500 years old; this tree was declared of historical and cultural heritage. She sighed and said, "This tree is so old with as much history; it is like an eternal tree". He kneels under the tree in front of Allegria, takes the ring out of his pocket and says: "My beloved, will you marry me?" He takes her hand and says, "Like this tree is eternal. I want our love to be and last for more than a thousand years". She sighs and smiles with emotion, tears rolling down her cheeks, but she manages to reply, "Yes, of course, my love, my true love!"

At once three tenors appear singing "Chiudo gli occhi e penso a lei, il profumo dolce della pelle sua, é una voce dentro che mi sta portando dove nasce il sole, sole sono le parole, ma se vanno scritte tutto puó cambiare, senza piú te lo voglio urlare questo grande amore... Amore, solo amore é quello che sento, dimmi perché quando penso, penso solo a te, dimmi perché quando vedo, vedo solo a te, dimmi perché quando credo, credo solo in te grande amore, dimmi che mai, che non mi lascerai mai, dimmi chi sei, respiro del giorni miei d'amore, dimmi che sai, che solo me sceglierai, ora lo sai, tu sei il sei il unico grande amore".

All those passers on the street stopped to see such a beautiful spectacle and applauded with emotion. Giovanni whispers in Allegria's ear: "tu sei il mio unico grande amore". She kissed him and could only thank God; she could not believe she was so happy. Of course, that night had to be celebrated, so everyone went to the restaurant on the corner, "Millennium", to mangiare e bere del buon vino. There was an atmosphere of total joy; they dined tortellini, cancelli, cappelletti, and sorrentino and drank the best Giordano wine from Puglia.

They were happy; they were all pleased.

***

One year later, they married in the Sct. Hans Kirke, the church that witnessed this love. The whole town went to the wedding; they had travelled to see their beloved Allegria's wedding. The Sisters of Charity made her the dress. It was a dream wedding, Cinderella-style.

The church was radiant, full of flowers, light, and joy. The choir delighted those present, and there were only words of love and happiness.

Allegria looked beautiful, and Giovanni was splendid with his princely bearing. The decoration was white, with cream colours such as light blue, light pink and light purple combined with cream and soft gold. They celebrated all night with a big banquet. It was a wonderful evening. Insurmountable.

They lived happily ever after in Denmark because dreams can come true.

God had changed all mourning into deep joy; Allegria went on to live the destiny of her name; she was eternally happy and pleased already in heaven. Giovanni's name and her name were written in heaven, and no one could take them away from that destiny; they were in the hands of God.

Giovanni brought balance to Allegria's life. This fantastic, beautiful, and exemplary man brought only good to her life. Allegria was the most blessed woman; she had found an actual prince.

Allegria was free forever, happy forever… what more could she desire in her life?

Love had won; true love had won. When you let God's will be done in your life, God always gives you the best because He only has great things to provide you.

As Cicero said, "Ut sementem feceris, ita metes", which means "What you sow will be what you reap." Giovanni and Allegria had sown good things, attitudes and a life of virtue, so only good things were in store for them now. Her harvest time had come. God had blessed them, and they were happy and pleased.

Time passed, and some people say that when Costantino got drunk, he would always sing "Payphone" by Maroon 5. They say it became his favourite song if we could say that Costantino had a favourite song.

Chapter 11
"O conscience, upright and stainless, how bitter a sting to thee is a little fault!"
Dante Alighieri

It was the year 2012. It had been 13 years since Allegria had moved to Denmark. She was married. They had two children with Giovanni Medici, and both made a comfortable, happy, traditional, and noble family. They were the only Medicis in Denmark. They raised their children by loving Jesus and following Lutheran traditions. They were pleased, and every day, they thanked God for being able to enjoy so much happiness. Such happiness could not fit into such bodies.

Suddenly the phone rang, and it was her friend Laura, with whom she had been in touch for all those years, and she was the one who had called to tell her the news.

Laura was crying about her father's death. Allegria was a good friend and told her she would travel to be with her during this challenging period. Allegria takes the first flight to Milano and then takes the train to Aosta, where Laura and the whole Mancini family are.

Allegria arrived just in time for the funeral, so she drove to the cemetery. Once she got off the train, Allegria passed through the arch of Augustus; what a beautiful feeling it gave her to be back in her city!

However, she didn't have time for so many contemplations; she had to arrive before 10:00 A.M. when the farewell liturgy would be celebrated.

The Aosta cemetery is impressive. It leaves you with a glimmer of solemnity because it makes you think of eternity with a mixture of art. After all, many sculptures were made for families that were part of the history of Aosta. An outstanding characteristic of this graveyard was the family's coat of arms. It is a mixture of nature, history, art, and eternity.

Allegria loved Aosta. She loved being in that city, but when she came to visit the holy field of Aosta, she felt uneasy, as if she had a feeling that something was going to happen.

She decided not to pay attention to these suspicions and continued to move forward. As she entered that field and looked around at the tombs, she began to hear some horror screams and hellish sayings; she could see some of those souls in hell.

It was like starting all that experience of that spiritual world coming back to visit her. She saw some souls groaning in pain at the bottom of hell; these souls were naked in the lake of fire and were crying out for help.

She tried to keep her composure and get to where her friend Laura and the whole Mancini family were.

When she arrives, she listens to the priest speak and repeat Psalm 23 for a farewell to Laura's father, Signore Flavio Mancini.

The priest read: "Il Signore é il mio pastore: non manco di nulla; su pascoli erbosi mi fa reposare ad acque tranquille mi conduce. Mi rinfranca, mi guida per il giusto cammino, per amore del suo nome. Se dovessi camminare in una valle oscura, non temerei alcun male, perché tu sei con me. Il tuo bastone e il tuo vincastro mi danno sicurezza. Davanti a me tu prepari una mensa sotto gli occhi dei miei nemici; cospargi di olio il mio capo. Il mio calice trabocca. Felicità e grazia mi saranno compagne tutti i giorni della mia vita, e abiterò nella casa del Signore per lunghissimi anni".

Then, to finish, the priest suggests that everyone repeat the Our Father's prayer.

"Padre nostro, che sei nei cieli, sia santificato il tuo nome; venga il tuo regno; sia fatta la tua volontà come in cielo così in terra. Dacci oggi il nostro pane cotidiano e rimetti i nostri debiti como anche noi li abbiamo rimettiamo ai nostri debitori e non abbandonarci alla tentazione ma liberaci dal male, perché tuo é il regno e la potenza e la gloria, per sempre, Amen".

Then the priest says: "Andate in pace". Everyone walks around, throwing a flower on the coffin. It was the last goodbye to a person as dear as Signore Flavio.

Allegria hugs Laura to give her strength. They walk and talk once all the people are gone, catching up on Aosta's latest news. Laura told her about the last days of her father's life, who fought against cancer and eventually lost the battle.

Suddenly, they stop, and Allegria sees a tombstone of someone she had known very well. The tombstone read:

"Costantino Habsburg

January 12, 1967
May 5, 2015
Riposa in pace".
Allegria was astonished and asked Laura, "How did he die?" Laura sighed and replied, "They found his body. It was on the news, and it was an apparent suicide. The police say he committed suicide. He had been living in depression in the last few years, and in the end, he ended his life".

Allegria was absorbed and exclaimed: "I didn't think he would ever have that ending". Laura nodded: "Come on, Allegria, with the life he led, I think that was the only possible end".

Then Allegria sadly replied, "He didn't want to accept God's forgiveness; he went too far from good". Laura, a sceptic woman, replied, "He didn't want to accept anyone's advice; in the end, that was the only end that awaited him".

They were both silent and headed out of the cemetery. Sadness overwhelmed them. It was a day of farewell! They had bid farewell to a parent and then saw someone they had both cherished once resting in peace.

***

Since Allegria was in Aosta, she took the opportunity to visit her parents. She always used to see them; sometimes Allegria's parents travel to Denmark, and other times, she and Giovanni come to see them and Giovanni's parents. However, Giovanni's parents lived in Florence; they divided the days between Aosta and Florence.

Allegria comes home, hugs her parents and says with surprise to her father: "Dad, have you heard what happened to Costantino?" The father nods and says, "Yes, it's unfortunate news; it's such sad news that we didn't want to talk about it since we do respect Costantino's parents; you know, he killed himself, perhaps because of the life he led. Deciding to follow all the evil things it was like committing suicide before society; then, he committed a true suicide. He had embraced evil, daughter; he embraced all evil; no one can come out of that life alive".

Allegria nods as she takes a cup of coffee from her father and asks Alberto to keep telling her how it all happened.

Allegria asks her father, "How did it happen? How was it?". Alberto closes his eyes and says: "Oh, daughter, you don't want to know; it's unfortunate!" Allegria insisted, showing strong confidence, "Come on, dad, I'm a grown-up; of course, I can handle this kind of thing!".
The father meditates briefly and says, "Well, all right, I'll tell you". Allegria pours more coffee, and the father narrates Costantino's story.
"Daughter, we know that sin is the absence of goodness, of order, a lawless life, a life of injustice and in the last years of his life, Costantino gave himself completely to that lifestyle, to the shadow. Since sin is like poison, it takes over everything; how can we make a person stop that poison if he loves the poison he consumes? Only God can bring a cure, but Costantino was not the kind of man who wanted to be cured. Costantino loved the poison; he loved being killed little by little. Hell welcomes sinners as heroes, but it becomes impossible to get out of there. The decisions one makes in life lead the soul to a specific destination. Choosing the path of blessing or curse determines where one will spend eternity; there is no way in between".
Allegria sighs and says sadly, "I'm sorry about what happened". Her father says, "Don't feel sorry; you were saved; Kennedy was surprisingly cruel to his wife; Costantino was also cruel to you; you are blessed daughter; you had let him go on time". Allegria nodded and said, "Yes, that's true, Father, but it's a pity that his life ended that way; committing suicide must be outrageous". Her father says, "You understand that his family had taken over everything in this city, everything they represent; you had been blessed, daughter, since you had separated yourself from everything… you are free; you came out of hell!".
Allegria, delighted by her father's words, said, "My beloved father, you are right on that, thanks". Then her father added, "Daughter, in life, the important thing is to live life fully and in a good way. Costantino forgot about respect for God, goodness, and righteousness; you are blessed since you had managed to break free from such a destructive influence as he was".
Father's words moved Allegria since they had never had such a conversation on this matter before, so she said, "My beloved

father, every day I thank God for being free and living in paradise. I thank God that he had mercy on me".

Then her father said, "In the last days of his life, Costantino was a strange man; after all, that was Costantino, a weirdo. Daughter, remember you told me that in Costantino's house was the painting of Bruno Amadio… it might seem like a hunch, but consider the hell that broke out in his house, as if hell had come to claim for his soul".

Allegria sighs with disbelief and says to her father, "Oh, dad, come on! You will not believe that a work of art can unleash misfortune on you, will you?" her father firmly replies: "A work that is consecrated to the darkness, of course, yes, they are gates that invite destruction. I don't think you who had seen the spiritual world would reject that". Allegria blushes and responds, "Yes, Dad, it's true because the whole spiritual world is more real than the material world; I've seen it… I've watched as people were on their way to hell. I've been there, but thank God that's past; my soul now rests in the best place: in heaven; what more could I ask from God?"

Silence filled the atmosphere. The father sipped some of his coffee and continued, "Daughter, Costantino, the last time, was no longer a man; he was an androgen, he was sick, he had become a binary or something like that, and you know that spirits attract each other, all kinds of destructive people surrounded him, demons know how to seduce each other. But thank God your soul had been cleansed because I know that the worst thing about having been with a person like him is the results of your soul, but thank God, you are already healthy; God had set you free". Allegria nods and says to her father, "Of course, that was the best blessing I have had, to heal me from all that hell, to get rid of all that hell. Only Jesus could restore me; only He could restore the soul".

Her father hugs and comforts her, "You came out of hell; I'm so glad for you; the passport out of hell is Jesus". Allegria agrees and replies, "Yes, dad, I missed talking to you and hearing your wisdom."

Her father caresses Allegria and exclaims, "Costantino fell in love with the darkness; for him, that was the perfect hell. But you must thank God for having come out of all that because you are part of the light… and the light belongs to heaven".

Allegria hugged her father; she was so happy to have such a good and wise father. Allegria felt exhausted; she had lived a long day and needed some sleep, so she said goodbye to her parents and went to her room to fall asleep, the one that used to belong to her when she was younger.

***

When she came into the room, so many memories came back to her. Her tender years, her childhood, her adolescence; she smiled with nostalgia. Now, she was quite a woman, but somewhere in that room was the little girl she was.

She puts on her pyjamas, brushes her teeth and goes to bed. The trip, the cemetery, all that news. She was exhausted.

She was utterly asleep until the angel of death visited her amid her deep sleep. He was dressed in a black robe, giant, enormous, taller than a skyscraper, he smelled of sulfur, on his head you could see his skull, he had no eyes, but he stared at Allegria, and she was frightened. Smoke was coming out of his feet. It was shocking, terrifying.

Allegria, frightened, stands still and is told, "Come with me; I have the order to show you something. Your God gave me the order to show you a soul". She obeys and follows him, even though she is afraid, but she knows she must trust God on the day she is scared. She knew God would want to show her something, so she obeyed. Her body had been left lying in the room; only her spirit was walking behind the angel of death.

Once again, screams, torture, afflictions, and despair begin to be felt everywhere.

Allegria reproaches and says, "No, I don't want to go down; I don't want to see what you are going to show me". The angel of death insists and says, "I was commanded to show you what you are going to see". The flames of fire cleared for a moment, and Allegria saw Costantino, full of pus, with worms gnawing at his bones, full of sores, with tears in his eyes, spitting blood, deeply depressed, hopeless, with chains on his hands and feet; a horrific scene.

Allegria, moved by an instinct of piety, rushed to see him and said, "Costantino, what have they done to you?" Costantino, crying, replied: "What have they done to me, not esteemed? What have I done to myself? Look, contemplate my eternity; I have no way out!" And began to cry deep tears of pain and repentance.

Allegria wants mercy to embrace him but can't. Then she asks him, "Are you alone here?" Costantino replies, "I'm all alone, nobody here with me, none of my friends who accompanied me to do my evil deeds, nobody's here. I only have hours of pain and suffering left. Allegria, how could I have been so wrong? How could I have missed the right path so much? I know it is very late, but I am so sorry". Allegria wept because seeing a human in such a situation was sad.

Allegria replied, "Costantino, that's life; you can choose the path you want; what you can't avoid are the results; every decision we make in life has eternal consequences and those results we can't alter; that's the law. The law comes to pass sooner or later". Costantino sadly exclaims, "This is already my real world; I can't alter it; I can't get out of here anymore". As he lamented as he wept bitterly, he wept as when someone had lost all hope; he cried as when a child had lost his home and his parents.

Allegria wept momentarily and said, "I had tried to warn you, to show you the right way. Still, you loved darkness more than light, and I see that your life was already overcome by the darkness. God knows I tried; I sincerely tried". Costantino hits his head and says; "I know, I know... but I was a fool".

Allegria just replies, "The one who practices sin is the devil, and you loved all that life of sin; that's why the darkness ravaged your life, and you decided to kill yourself," Costantino says: "I didn't decide to kill myself, I don't know how it was, I was in ecstasy, hell came looking for me, I was tired of living, so I decided to end it all, I thought that all the pain would end and the only thing that happened was that all the pain became stronger, here I don't have a second of rest, my soul is completely broken, my heart can no longer bear it, it was hell that came for me, I saw the demons hugging me and was already defeated, I knew that I was already defeated, maybe I was born for this... to lose myself", Allegria accuses him, "No, you were not born to lose yourself; you had decided to lose yourself".

There was a moment of silence between them as all the constant torments in the others were heard.

Costantino says, "Sin has claimed my soul, I have been deceived, sin charged me more than I thought it would pay. And look at me. I am finished, eternally finished". At that moment, Costantino breaks down and continues to cry without consolation.

After a few minutes of deep tears of regret, Costantino says to Allegria: "Go and tell everyone you know that hell is real; above all, go and tell my family so that all may be saved and no one may descend to this place... I know that I love darkness more than light. I know that I am guilty of all the punishments I receive, but please, go and tell everyone I know to take care of their relationship with God... the best-kept secret from hell is that they make us believe that one can live as one wishes and still go to heaven when in reality it is not so if one does not walk in fear before a true and holy God, one cannot be part of His Kingdom, and I know that it is too late. Still, I am so sorry, so deeply repentant".

Allegria sighs, wipes away her tears, and says, "It is very late, Costantino; you should have repented on earth, and you said it well, as the prophet Nathan said to King David: you are that man! You're that man who did so much wrong... but didn't want to regret it. We warned you that you were heading for perdition and didn't listen to us; I know it's late, but I'm sorry that everything happened the way it did".

Costantino remained silent and said, "Yes, I know I am that man... I neglected my relationship with God, the fear of God inside me went out, and nothing remained".

Costantino goes on to say, "Allegria, you were always a heroine, you were always my heroine, you were always better than me... they say that heroism usually coexists with lack of love", Allegria says, "No Costantino, I tried to help you. Still, I was never a heroine, so I know how to coexist with love, with the love of a person as human as myself, I came out of your clutches and found what I was looking for, after all, what communion does light have with darkness? You always represented the darkness; I always loved the light" Costantino weeps and says "Yes, I know, I suppose that everything in life must be like that; one is free of something bad to find something better", Allegria concludes, "Yes, I suppose it is like that... well, I must leave you, that's all, goodbye Costantino."

Allegria wore glowing clothes because she belonged to heaven, but she felt the heat of hell and being there made her feel nauseous. She wanted to get out of there, and the whole experience lasted so much while it particles of seconds in the real world. But again, what union can light have with darkness? When you belong to heaven, you want nothing to do with hell.

Allegria saw with her own eyes that the price of sin is death; it is the death of all that is good and beautiful... it is the death of the soul. Costantino was alive in hell but without anything good or beautiful to enjoy; eternal death already possessed his whole soul.

Allegria has realized once again that everything the enemy of our souls sells you is a total lie, a deception; the shadow makes you believe that your life would be fantastic; it gives you a false identity, gives you a wrong space, gives you wrong wisdom making you think that you are more intelligent than others in making your way, a false sense of authority to believe that you are the only one to do it your way and a wrong circle of friends who applaud all your foolish decisions.

When it comes time to pay the price, you are alone, and without anyone, you are before your actual reality, only you before eternity. Allegria could see how all those false friends had disappeared; no one was there; Costantino was alone... alone in flames dying of so much pain, with so much remorse and condemnation.

With his last breath, Costantino took his strength to say; "Allegria, wait! If I came back to life, I would do everything differently, I would do everything in a different way; I am so sorry". Allegria looked at him with compassion and said, "I understand... but it's too late, it's too late to apologize".

Right away, the gate of hell is closed forever.

Costantino cried without consolation, moaning in pain; tears were running out... he was in hell, and the only thing he had left was lament.

Allegria only repeated, "It's too late... too late."

As that famous One Republic and Timbaland song "I'm holding on your rope, got me ten feet off the ground, and I'm hearing you say, but I just can't make a sound, you tell me that you need me, then you do and cut me down but wait, you tell me that you're sorry, didn't think I'd turn around, and say... that it's too late to apologize, it's too late, I said it's too late to apologize, it's too late. I'd take another chance, take a fall, take a shot for you, and I need you like a heart needs a beat, but it's nothing new; yeah, yeah, I loved you with a fire red, and now it's turning blue, and you say sorry like the angel, heaven let me think were you. But I'm afraid... that it's too late to apologize, it's too late; I said it's too late to apologize, it's too late to apologize. I'm holding on your rope, got me ten feet off the ground".

***

That's the end of Costantino's life. He leaves no offspring. He opposed God; he opposed His law, he opposed the truth, and that's why his life ended ruined; he ended up as King Saul's life ended, someone who had everything to shine and ended up in the deepest darkness, as 1 Chronicles 10:13-14 related: "Saul died because he was unfaithful to the Lord; he did not keep the word of the Lord and even consulted a medium for guidance, and did not inquire of the Lord. So the Lord put him to death and turned the kingdom over to David son of Jesse".

As it happened with Costantino's life, he consulted and flirted with the whole hidden world, the world of darkness; that's why everything was taken away from him, and everything that belonged to him ended up belonging to someone else. To another person with a better heart than his.

We will all have to appear before the law of God sooner or later, and we will not be able to give excuses that we weren't aware of our wrongdoings because we will all undoubtedly receive the weight of the law and be accountable to it. That is why we must make peace with Jesus so that we will only receive mercy the day we face the direction.

The heart of Costantino was evil, as was that of King Jeroboam, because so many times Costantino had the opportunity to repent but never wanted to listen, as 1 Kings 13:33 and 34 says, "Even after this, Jeroboam did not change his evil ways, but once more appointed priests for the high places from all sorts of people. Anyone who wanted to become a priest he consecrated for the high places. This was the sin of the house of Jeroboam that led to its downfall and to its destruction from the face of the earth".

Jeroboam always did what he wanted: his laws and rules; he never respected the authority of God, the law of God, just like Costantino. That's why his name was also ripped off. Nobody talked about him anymore; nobody remembered him anymore. It's just that there was nothing good to talk about or remember.

Allegria woke up and came to her senses. She understood that she had seen a vision and that it was goodbye to the ugliest chapter of her life.

She had a mixture of sensations because she knew that her present and future were promising, at the same time regretting what she saw with her own eyes; it was such a sad ending, but it was announced.

That morning at breakfast, she told her father what she dreamed of. Her father tells her as a secret confession that Costantino's parents wept bitterly at the end of his son's life. They remember Prince Absalom, who was born in a golden cradle and had everything to reign, but he rebelled against his father, King David, and this caused his death.

King David grieved bitterly over the death of his Son Absalom, just like Costantino's parents cried.

"The king asked the Cushite, "Is the young man Absalom safe?" The Cushite replied, "May the enemies of my lord the King and all who rise up to harm you be like that young man." The King was shaken. He went up to the room over the gateway and wept. As he went, he said: "O, my son Absalom! My son, my son Absalom! If only I had died instead of you –O Absalom, my son, my Son!" (2 Samuel 18:32 to 33).

It was the farewell of a friend to a friend. Allegria decided to go to the cemetery and bring some flowers; she wore a beautiful little black suit, which evoked the 1950s. She took a handful of yellow flowers and took them away.

She took a little piece of paper that she had written and read it in front of the tomb: "May you rest Costantino, the Bible says: 'Whoever has the Son has life; whoever does not have Son of God does not have life', I regret that everything ended as it ended in your life, you had chosen hell, I have chosen heaven. Goodbye, friend, and rest in peace", and then she whispers, "If you can".

She left the letter under the bouquet and decided to leave. She never came back. She never visited that place again. Her life was beautiful. There was no reason to go back to that place. She left without looking back. She went off to live her life, the wonderful life that was waiting for her. She never thought she could be so happy. She came out of hell forever, and she thanked God daily for this.

Allegria went on to live her life; she got out of hell, and only those who were in agony and came out of there know what it means to "be alive and out of there". Allegria was free from torment, huge affliction, and anguish; do you know what it means to be free from all that? It's priceless; there are no words.

Costantino never understood that it was not what he felt or did, but what God said it was; he believed all the lies the system sold him and ended up like this: finished. Costantino never knew how to appropriate the identity God gave him and be free to fulfil his purpose, the destiny God had created for him.

Allegria came out of hell because God is merciful, because she clung to God and God, in his immense mercy, had compassion on her, forgave her for her bad decisions and brought her out of the depths of the abyss.

We never lose in the kingdom of God because what seemed so damaging to Allegria's life was her greatest blessing. She finally won. God delivered her from the power of her enemies. Her enemies could no longer touch her; she was in another realm, another atmosphere. She was free and had come out of all the torment. All her enemies lost total power over her, and she was free... free to live a peaceful life.

What seemed at first to be a significant loss in Allegria's life ended up being her biggest prize.

Throughout the liberation process, Allegria learned to break her will and understood that God's will is always much better than hers and that God's thoughts are always much better, higher and more sublime than hers. She learned to trust in God and to obey by doing His will.

By obeying, she became as happy as she could ever have imagined.

Allegria understood that only God is the source of life, and in his light, we can see the light, as Psalm 36:9 says, "For with you is the fountain of life; in your light do we see the light". No more

darkness; now, her life was full of light, and Allegria loved that light.
The day Allegria left hell, she left for good and never went back there, never had contact with it again.
Now her life was complete.

Chapter 12
"For God, in giving Himself that man might be able to raise himself, gave even more that if he had forgiven him in mercy".
Dante Alighieri

Everywhere in the world, we can see a few paintings with a copy of the famous dome of Florence's cathedral, designed by the genius of the Renaissance, Filippo Brunelleschi.

Florence is a city known worldwide for its artistic and architectural heritage. Its historic centre was declared a World Heritage Site by UNESCO in 1982.

It was a significant cultural, economic, and financial centre in the Middle Ages. It was at its most splendid after the establishment of the Grand Duchy of Tuscany under the rule of the Medici dynasty.

Giovanni de Medici founded this dynasty. He was not born rich, and the little money left by his father, Averardo, must have been divided between the widow and five children. He was a hard-working, simple man, always on a mule.

Giovanni was interested in politics regarding what might affect his bank business. Giovanni was the head of the family bank, representing his main commercial interest, operating across the city-states of northern Italy and beyond.

Giovanni de Medici approached Baltassare Crossa and offered him his support and the backing of his bank on his way to the papacy. In 1410 Crossa became John XXIII, and as a reward for his help, the Medici Bank became the church's bank. After the abdication of John XXIII, the successive popes continued to use the services of the Medici Bank. He also enjoyed the privilege of collecting agricultural taxes and the right to exploit several alum deposits.

Then his son Cosimo di Giovanni de Medici, that is, Cosimo, continued with the dynasty. He married Contessima Bardi, who belonged to another family of bankers. As a member of War Ten, Cosimo opposed the oligarchic regime established in Florence, where the Albizzi family's rival family prevailed.

Cosimo's influence, endowed with a unique political sense, became even more critical when the head of the oligarchy, Rinaldo degli Albizzi, had him arrested in 1433 on embezzlement charges. He was imprisoned in Palazzo Vecchio and sent into exile for ten years. Cosimo settled in Venice, with the support of Pope Eugene IV, without losing contact with the partisans.

The partisans were the fighters organized as guerrillas who opposed the Albizzi occupation or resisted their government.

Albizzi maintained a brutal confrontation with his enemies; neither his prestige nor his money intimidated his opponents; a year later, in 1434, Cosimo got his sentence annulled, so he returned to Florence. Triumphant and acclaimed by the people, he banished his rival. Like his father, he was appointed Gonfaloniere of Florence during the same year, a civilian position allowing him to carry out his political wishes.

He was trying to turn his family into the justice of the Florentine state. To this end, and in different directions, he used his extraordinary fortune from the bank inherited from his father, who had subsidiaries in various Italian states and abroad. To this end, he pursued a successful foreign policy and established a peaceful relationship with enemy states such as the Duchy of Milan. He promoted foreign policy and exerted, through it, a significant influence throughout Italy. One of the constitutional reforms he carried out was the creation of 1458 of the Council of 100 at the proposal of banker Luca Pitti. He can be considered the man who earned the most money in the Medici family's commercial enterprise.

He supported Brunelleschi in finishing the dome of Florence; this is the symbol in all of Florence of having triumphed over the impossible. He founded the Medici patronage, a lover of art and science; he put his fortune at their service with the generosity of a great lord, and all of Florence followed his example; although he could not write literature, he made several contributions to the preservation of libraries. For instance, as a gift to the Florentine philosopher Marsilio Ficino, he gave the town of Careggi to study Plato's thoughts. He was a great collector and, inspired by his interest in artistic production, was advised by Donatello, with whom he became friends; he encouraged him in his creative acquisitions.

Cosimo received the collection from his assistant and librarian Niccolo Niccoli and deposited it in a room in the convent of San Marco in Florence designed by Michelozzo in 1441. This was the first of his donations to churches and convents, and then he erected the novitiate of Santa Croce and invested in the reconstruction of San Lorenzo. Cosimo's magnificence was modelled on divine excellence in his monasteries and churches. One of the characteristics of his patronage was to combine construction companies with the obtaining of humanist books. However, in private constructions, it was moderated, since until 1444, he had his palace remodelled, leaving the previous decoration. He chose Michelozzi's most modest project; the court had a façade with characteristics of the medieval tradition and was completed in 1460. He also created the Library of St. George the Elder in Venice and the Abbey of Fiesole.

The dynasty fell on Lorenzo Medici, also known as Lorenzo the Magnificent by his contemporaries. He was a statesman and de facto ruler of the Republic of Florence, in Italian, Firenze. Lorenzo was a prince of Florence, patron of the arts, diplomat, banker, poet and Renaissance philosopher. His life coincided with the height of the early Italian Renaissance; his death marks the end of the Golden Age of Florence. The fragile peace he helped to maintain between the various Italian states ended with his death. Lorenzo's remains rest in the Medici Chapel in the Basilica of St. Lawrence in Florence.

Lorenzo was first educated in Venice and then sent to Milan at nineteen on behalf of his father. While still young, his father sent him to numerous diplomatic missions. These include visiting Rome to see the Pope and other political and religious figures.

At age twenty, in 1469, his father's death forced him to take charge of the Florentine state under a permanent pulse with the Kingdom of Naples. The confrontations between the heads of the family of the Florentine Republic kept the city in tension, and Lorenzo had to dispute his position permanently. His conciliatory and diplomatic character allowed him to achieve peace with the Neapolitans in 1480 after the war between Ferdinand I of Naples was declared.

Some historians consider him a maintainer of order in a very turbulent period in the history of Italian cities. The confrontation between the Medici and the Pazzi, another influential banking family of the town, continued throughout their principality. They had to suffer at least two attacks, the most famous of which occurred on April 26, 1478, the Pazzi conspiracy, which took place in front of the Florence Duomo on a Sunday of mass. In this crazy operation, the Pazzi family took the life of Lorenzo's younger brother, Giuliano.

Lorenzo married one of the noblest women of the Roman aristocracy, Clarissa Orsini. He succeeded in getting his son to make a career as a clergyman so that he would later become Pope Leo X.

As a patron of the arts, he supported artists such as Sandro Botticelli, Leonardo da Vinci, Giuliano da Maiano, and Michelangelo. He spread Italian Renaissance art throughout the rest of the European courts thanks to his excellent relations.

He founded, among other institutions, the Laurentian Library. Lorenzo's envoys recovered many classical works from Eastern Europe, setting up workshops to copy his books and disseminate their contents throughout Europe.

The Medicis transformed Florence. They changed the world. They created economic mobility and broke cycles. Something different happened to them. Before the Medici, if one were born poor, one would remain poor lifetime. They created the middle class, that there could be a social dynamic and that you could change your generation no matter your family.

They introduced the idea of changing the dynamics and generating an economic movement, the famous "middle class". They had the most prosperous bank in all of Europe. This family shocked the whole of Europe; it was one of the most politically influential families on the continent and dominated all of Florence for three centuries. It was the most powerful family in all of Europe.

It was a family of humble origins but became more prosperous than the Rockefellers, more potent than the Borgias and more influential than the Kennedys.

60% of the world's art is found in Italy, of which 40% is produced in Italy by a single family: the Medici. On a world scale, 25% of universal art produced by just one family is accounted for by 25%, which is not bad for a single family that came out of the shadows of the unknown.

A family that made names like Donatello, Niccolò Machiavelli, Leonardo da Vinci, the absolute genius of Filippo Brunelleschi (an engineer who is still being studied today because they cannot understand how he built the dome of the Cathedral of Santa Maria di Fiore, his mind was astonishing), Sandro Botticelli, Francesco Petrarca, Giovanni Boccaccio, Giorgio Vasari who created the first book in the history of art producing the term "rinascita" which means "rebirth," the most outstanding scientist of all times: Galileo Galilei and the most significant artist humanity has ever had; Michelangelo Buonarroti.

The Medici gave the best to Europe and the world, and although they also had to endure the worst, they shared so many good things in so little time.

A family that came out of selling wool and ended up giving the Catholics three Popes: Leo X, Clement VII and Leo XI; two queens of France, Catherine de Medici and Mary de Medici; members of the royal houses of France and England and the world remembers them for having been the most significant patron saints in history to have sheltered such magnificent artists and scientists.

They expanded from Florence to the world, from the fantastic Florence to the world.

The Medicis had made themselves rich and powerful with hard work. They came from below, they were not born to reign, but they managed to reign.

The Habsburgs had everything they needed to rule, but as with Costantino, they did not even reach the height of a crown diamond. The Medicis were born with nothing and came to have all the crowns, and the kingdom, as was the case with Giovanni, did not have so much but ended up having everything. Because in this life, what is important is not how or where you are born but what you do. Character determines your destiny.

Giovanni developed discipline, holiness, honour, and great virtues… that's why he got the whole kingdom to reach the top of the dream. Costantino did not develop good qualities in his life; there was no discipline, and looking at the results, he ruined his life.

Oscar Wilde, an Irish playwright and novelist, would describe it, "Every little action of the common day makes or unmakes character" and how he was so wisely defined by the Roman dramatic poet Pubilio Siro; "His own character is the arbiter of everyone's fortune".

Character.

Giovanni had character, but Costantino didn't. And after all, who wants a Habsburg if you have a Medici?

The Italy of the Quattrocento and Cinquecento, with the Medicis in command of all of Florence, produced great painters such as Vasari, Bronzino, Pontormo, Andrea del Sarto, Fra Bartolommeo, Michelangelo, Rafael, Leonardo da Vinci, Perugino, Signorelli, Girlandaio, Masaccio, Giotto, Botticelli, Andrea Verrochio, Fra Angelico, Filippino Lippi, and Piero della Francesca.

Sculptors include Giacomo della Porta, Giovanni da Bologna, Michelangelo, Desiderio, Leonardo da Vinci, Donatello, Giotto, and Antonio Pollaiuolo.

Architects such as Vasari, Arnolfo Di Cambio, Michelangelo, Sangallo, Bramante, Leonardo da Vinci, the genius of Brunelleschi, Alberti, Giotto, and Filarete, among others.

Writers such as Dante, Poliziano, Leonardo da Vinci, Boccaccio, and Machiavelli.

Throughout Florence, you can see the Medicis' hand, such as the dome of Santa Maria del Fiore, the Ponte Vecchio, the Basilica of Santa Croce, the Palazzo Vecchio and museums such as the Uffizi, the Bargello or the Gallery of the Academy, which houses the David of Michelangelo.

These beautiful minds made Florence a city known worldwide for its artistic and architectural heritage. The most widespread artistic style in the town is the Renaissance, created in the same city in the second half of the 14th century. However, it also has an important heritage of other architectural and artistic styles.

The heart of the city is Piazza della Signoria, where the Palazzo Vecchio, the city's administrative centre since medieval times, the Loggia dei Lanzi and the nearby Uffizi Gallery, one of the most important museums in Italy, are located. A few minutes away from this square is Piazza del Duomo, whose centre is the Basilica of Santa Maria del Fiore, Florence's cathedral and known for its dome, a Renaissance masterpiece designed by the genius of Filippo Brunelleschi.

The Campanile di Giotto and the Baptistery of San Giovanni complete the monumental complex of Piazza del Duomo.

Practically this magnificent city was generated by the Medicis.

Two significant figures within the Medicis were Cosimo and Lorenzo: Father and Son.

Cosimo went on to support Brunelleschi in constructing the cathedral in Florence. The cathedral, known in Italian as the Duomo, comes from the Latin "Domus Dei," which means "House of God". This cathedral is located in the heart of the old part of the city. It is famous for its large dome, which is 45 m in diameter and 100 m high. This magnificent work was carried out by the genius of Brunelleschi, one of the greatest architects ever produced by humanity. To this day, science cannot explain how he did the work he did without the technology we have today. It's a mystery.

There are frescoes by Giorgio Vasari inside the cathedral representing the final judgment. The building, of gigantic dimensions, is of a Latin cross with a central nave and two lateral naves. The floor is covered with coloured marble, forming a labyrinth of shapes and textures. Except for the dome and the orange ceramic roofs, the temple walls are covered with white, green and pink Tuscan marble.

A characteristic of many Italian temples is that the bell tower is not attached to the church, but separated, a few meters from it. Giotto designed it, completely covered with brightly coloured Tuscan marble.

Just in front of the cathedral is the excellent baptistery. The most famous part of the baptistery is the gates on the east side, also known as the Gates of Paradise, designed by Ghiberti. They are decorated with gilded bronze bas-reliefs, including a self-portrait of the artist.

Can you imagine what an extraordinary feeling a Florentine had when he visited such a large church that was the city's glory? When everyone arrived in Florence, they could see the dome, the cathedral, and the Duomo, which seemed to reveal the greatest treasure of God here on earth.

Cosimo was happy with what he had accomplished.

Cosimo's heir, Lorenzo, was different. Lorenzo's patronage consisted not so much in financing works as Cosimo did but in sending the most outstanding artists of Florence (Botticelli, the Pollaiolo to Rome, Maiano to Naples, Sansovino to Lisbon, Verrocchio to Venice, etc.) to various courts, practising the "politics of artistic prestige". His taste and criteria were highly valued because he endowed with a great sensitivity demonstrated by his poems; he liked to surround himself with artists, philosophers and scientists: he loved the contact with intelligence and talent as if to cultivate in himself a kind of universal artist, to acquire or to sense all the virtues of genius.

Some scholars proclaim Lorenzo as one of the "godfathers of the Renaissance". He founded the so-called "sculpture garden," with which he sought to revive the art of sculpture, which was almost extinct in Florence. In this garden, free teaching was given in the process of sculpting the most talented apprentices in the workshops of the time, including the young Michelangelo, and it was there that he made several of his first marble works, such as The Virgin of the Stairs and The Battle of the Centaurs.

To fill the need for a master sculptor in the sculpture garden, Lorenzo hired Bertoldo, a former apprentice of the famous sculptor Donatello, who in turn had been Ghiberti's apprentice.

Despite his advanced age, Bertoldo taught the art of marble sculpting to his garden apprentices, giving them the foundation to revive sculpture in Florence.

Now, death comes to all of us, Cosimo died in peace, but Lorenzo did not; they say that even before his last breath, Lorenzo feared death.

What if God didn't like his life's work? What if God rejected him? What if his destiny was hell?

When you approach the end time of your life, you want to obtain all that money cannot buy, which is the absolution of all your sins.

In the last years of Lorenzo's life, a prophet named Girolamo Savonarola rose in Florence.

Savonarola preached against the luxury, the profit, the depravity of the powerful and the corruption of the church, against the pursuit of glory and sodomy, indicating that all these evils prevailed in Florence's society.

As our society is today throughout the world.

Savonarola had visions and was a prophet of God. He predicted that a new king, Cyrus, would cross the country to bring order to the customs of the priests and the people. Let us remember that Cyrus passed through Babylon, destroying it. Babylon was the cradle of idolatry and perversion.

The entry of Charles VIII's French army into Tuscany in 1494 confirmed his prophecy.

Savonarola accused the Medici family of corruption. He attacked Pope Alexander VI, for which he was excommunicated and then imprisoned.

Later, after being freed and taken to Rome by the great Florentine merchants, a court of the Inquisition condemned him to the stake and included his work in the index of forbidden books.

Savonarola had come from a noble family, Bonacolsi, who were feudal lords in Mantua. His grandfather was a doctor and a famous author in medicine. Savonarola had an educated and cultured family; he had a well-off childhood and was highly educated to the best society could have given him at the time.

His grandfather was deeply religious, a Bible scholar, with simple and strict customs. He was a man of faith. His grandfather, along with his education and lifestyle, was what impacted Savonarola's formation.

His grandfather taught him grammar, music, drawing, and, most importantly, a life of faith and integrity.

It can be said that Savonarola was the faithful reflection of his grandfather. He knew the scriptures and could recite them by heart. He meditated on them constantly.

The habit of prayer accompanied him all his life. When he was a child, he practised praying, and then when he grew up, this habit grew, and he spent many hours praying. After growing up, he liked to be in the fields, alone, in silence, praying and meditating on the scriptures.

Savonarola turned to the teachings of St. Thomas. At 18, he dedicated himself to theology, studying Catholic doctrines. In 1472 he wrote "De ruina Mundi" and "De ruina Ecclesiae" in 1475, comparing the Pope's Rome to the ancient and corrupt Babylon.

He entered the convent of St. Augustine, where he became a priest. He then moved to the Dominican order and concentrated on studying theology. He wrote sermons in which he accused the church of all its sins. Humanist popes were his favourite targets.

Why humanist popes? Because the true God cannot share space with other gods. God in the book of Chronicles opposes certain kings because they left the altars in high places for the people to go and worship those other gods. God is not dictatorial; when God says "no", it is because He knows that such a thing will hurt us. Idolatry does total damage. Moral, spiritual, physical, and mental damage because it destroys the soul; for this reason, God is determining in saying, "I made you, I know what is best for your life, adore me because I formed you in your mother's womb, if you go after other gods the only thing they will do is hurt you because they will give you a wrong image of yourself, I formed you, I have the right and exact image of you".

The people listened to Savonarola, and he always called for a simple life and simple faith in his appeals. The Savonarola Masses brought together 15,000 people, a highly significant number for what was once Florence. There was no room for people in the church.

Savonarola held that all the evils of this world were due to lack of faith; for whoever had faith would immediately realize that it is necessary to do better because the sorrows of hell are infinite.

He stressed that only faith saves and, by being held, do good deeds. Savonarola preached that living a godly life here on earth was worth it because all the suffering in hell can't compare to the sorrows we might have by keeping a life apart from evil.

According to Savonarola, the powerful ones of this world were proud to have ended the simple life of previous centuries. According to him, the priests of these times were the worst because they did everything opposite to the Bible teachings and got away from how they should do it; they were only interested in the goods of this world, and they no longer cared for the souls and hearts of their people but were only concerned about making a profit.

Doesn't all this sound familiar? Doesn't Savonarola seem to you to be describing today's society?

In his preaching, he spoke of the modesty, sobriety, and strong character that true believers must have to fight evil. He became a teacher of studies. In his life in the convent, he was distinguished by his rigorous fasting and penance, practising absolute frugality, and eating and drinking very little.

He was primarily dedicated to emphasizing preaching after studying techniques for public speeches.

At age 34, he was given ownership of St. Mark's Church in Florence. His ardent preaching, full of prophetic warnings, was not strange then. Still, his prophecies seemed to be fulfilled by the disasters that the city of Florence was experiencing in those years, such as the defeat against the French or the excessive luxury of the rich, who lived surrounded by works of art in front of thousands of people living in poverty. In these conditions, the population came to Savonarola because they denounced all these inequalities.

Another disaster was the syphilis epidemic. Many believed that Savonarola was the prophet of the "end times".

The church where Savonarola preached was known for its fanaticism. Savonarola did not preach doctrines; he preached about what it was like to live a Christian life. With his preaching, he was not trying to wage war against the Church of Rome, but he wanted to correct its sins.

He preached boldly, with the anointing of the Holy Spirit, and when people heard him, they were moved by their sins. As he preached, people sometimes cried, and sobs were heard as he taught the scriptures, so much so that people left the church silently and did not want to speak in the streets.

The most cultured men began to listen to his preaching. The rich began to correct their behaviour, helping the poor and helping them to sustain their families.

It is said that people would get up at night to go to church to wait for the door to be opened to enter. So many people had to wait to get in.

Savonarola believed that the Lord's day of vengeance was near. He continually fed his soul with the Word of God. His margins in the Bible were filled with notes that he wrote as he meditated on the scriptures. He knew much of the Bible by heart and found any text instantly. He made the Bible his instruction book.

He spent entire nights praying and had the grace to receive divine revelations. He had visions and came to see the heavens open and what calamities would happen inside the church. This was undoubtedly the case. All his prophecies were fulfilled.

He wept for the sins of Florence, and they say that when he rose from prayer, he left the altar wet with so many tears that he shed in favour of the people of Florence.

He stood out among the other monks and preachers for his humility, sincerity and obedience.

At that moment of height, when the people of Florence were listening to Savonarola, Lorenzo sent for him because he knew he was dying and would not survive much longer.

Like when you are overcome by fear or holy respect for God because you know your soul will go to the other world and not return. Lorenzo was afraid; he knew he was dying and had to ask God for forgiveness for his sins.

Everyone will have to answer to God sooner or later.

We will all face a perfect law.

We will all experience eternity because eternity lies within us. We will all live in our soul, and that soul will end up in one of those two places: heaven or hell.

Savonarola came to Lorenzo and said, "Lorenzo, do you have any sins to confess?".

We don't know what the conversation must have been like, but it didn't end well, and Lorenzo ended his days until his last breath, fearing hell.

Lorenzo ended up begging for everything that money couldn't buy; salvation.

When the hour of death comes, all you want is absolution from all your sins. As Jesus would wisely say, "What good will it be for someone to gain the whole world, yet forfeit their soul? Or what can anyone give in exchange for their soul?" (Matthew 16:26).

Because eternal life… is everlasting life of the soul, whether in heaven or hell. Savonarola wisely tried to convey this message and awaken the soul's consciousness throughout Florence.

When we go before the Judge of judges, the only thing that will matter is whether we have salvation and are all guilty of sin. No one is without sin; no one can throw the first stone.

Do you remember the famous case of O.J. Simpson; he was guilty and had all the evidence against him, but he was found "innocent" because he had the right group of lawyers to defend him, and for that reason, he was acquitted of guilt.

All of us are guilty before God; all of us have sinned; all of us have told a few lies; all of us have poorly thought of our neighbour; all of us have deceived; all of us have taken something that did not belong to us, and the list of sins can continue, but Jesus offered Himself to represent us as "Advocate" before a righteous judge.

God loves us but cannot ignore the evil we have done because he is fair, so we need Jesus, our true advocate in life. Only Jesus can defend us. We must confess to Him all that we have done wrong in life, humble ourselves, ask for forgiveness, and accept Him as our defender, saviour and master so that Jesus can defend us before a God of love who is also holy and fair.

We cannot judge others because God is the only true Judge. We can consider sin itself, but not the sinner. For example, a person with a bad attitude at a social gathering, we can say, "Yes, it's true, he has a bad attitude; it wasn't nice to talk to that person; he seemed angry", but we can't judge his heart, his person, maybe that person just got into a fight with his spouse, or he got bad news from his parents or one of his relatives is sick and so on, thousands of reasons that would explain the reason for that attitude.

You can point out sin but never to the sinner because we will never know the real reasons that hurt that heart.

Only God can judge wisely; only before God should every human being be accountable, and when that time comes, make sure you have Jesus as your advocate, able to absolve you of all your sins in such a way that God, the righteous Judge full of mercy, will declare you "innocent, saved".

Lorenzo was unsure whether or not he had Jesus on his side, and we don't know where his soul is; we don't know what the destiny of his soul was, heaven or hell. We can only say that he feared to the last breath to spend an eternity in hell.

We must make peace with God; today is an excellent day to reconcile with him.

When Savonarola was preaching to make peace with God before it was too late, Florence was invaded by the French king Charles VIII, who made him want to assert his right to rule Naples, so he decided to enter Italy with his army and pass through Florence.

Savonarola considered this act as being sent from heaven to bring order to the church, cleanse the impure from the heart, and rethink what was truly important: "salvation".

When Florence was invaded, the rebellion broke out. The rulers of the Medici family were accused and expelled. After the expulsion of the Medicis, Savonarola emerged as the city's leader and began to govern the strongly religious Democratic Republic of Florence.

Savonarola, in her eagerness to save everyone, tried humanly to pursue sin and evil and was against homosexuality, alcohol, gambling, and indecent clothing. Savonarola ordered the police to search the city for anything that would allow vanity or sin, such as gambling tables, erotic books and filthy clothing (women's dresses too low-cut, men's shorts too tight) to be confiscated by the police and thrown into the so-called "bonfire of vanities", a vast bonfire that burned in the main square of the city.

All Florentines were invited to throw objects that would drive them to sin.

Art itself is neither bad nor literature, music, cosmetics, or sex… the question is: "What motivates you to make a work of art? What promotes this art? What does it promote? What do you read? What is your real motivation for doing this or that?"

Not everything is wrong; what matters are the motivations behind that bias to action.

Botticelli, fearing for eternity, repented his many sins and even threw some of his works at the stake because he considered them harmful to the souls of others.

They threw at the stake licentious books like those of Giovanni Boccaccio, mythological paintings, books with profane poetry by Petrarca, and books they considered immoral.

As the 20-meter bonfire burned, people sang hymns and bells to announce victory.

People stopped reading banal books, started reading Savonarola's preaching, stopped singing worldly songs, and began praising God.

Savonarola had a genuine desire for everyone to turn to God, to return to simple customs and with some of his methods, he could have been wrong because, in this life, we cannot force anyone to give up sin. Still, the intention of his heart was genuine and reasonable; he wanted everyone to be saved.

While all this was happening, a group against the Savonarola government was formed, called the arrabbiata or the angry ones, who were defeated in the streets by the preacher's followers.

At that time, Savonarola continued to preach against sin, attacking the family of the pope, the family of the Borgias, and was now definitely at odds with the Duke of Milan and Pope Alexander VI.

Pope Alexander VI was irritated by so much criticism that he threatened all the inhabitants of Florence with the penalty of interdiction, which meant banning the sacraments for all citizens and preventing the dead from being buried in blessed cemeteries, as was customary in those years. These threats provoked terror among the people of Florence.

This causes Savonarola to fall into disgrace. Many of those who tried to protect him died. They wanted to silence him but could not; he returned to the pulpit and continued preaching against sin. The pope ordered his arrest and execution. By then, the King of France, Charles VIII, their most important defender, had passed away. The city does not resist, and the citizens will give up the friar. Savonarola and his friends Fray Domenico de Pescia and Fray Silvestro were arrested.

Savonarola was accused of heresy, rebellion, and religious errors and was imprisoned in Florence. For forty-two days, he was tortured, as well as his supporters. In the end, Savonarola signs his repentance with his right arm, which the torturers had left intact so that he could do so.

He regretted having signed the confession presented to him by his torturers and prayed to God that he would have mercy on his weakness, confessing to crimes he did not believe he had committed. On the day of his execution, he was still working on his book "Obsedit Me", which means "I am obsessed".

He was hanged and burned by order of the pope. He died saying, "The Lord suffered so much for me".

They burned him but failed to extinguish the truths he had captured in the hearts of the people.

His humility, love, and prayer books will continue influencing those who read them significantly. He was a holy man of integrity who sought all of Florence's salvation.

Yes, it's true, he had his mistakes, but his successes had overcome those wrongdoings.

Savonarola was a man of strong, charismatic character who sought the good of all Florence. Many compare him to Luther in his denunciation of the corruption of the Catholic Church. Still, he did not establish any doctrinal basis, unlike Luther himself, the forerunner of the Protestant schism. Savonarola was a foretaste of the moral reformation that Protestantism and the Counter-Reformation were to bring.

After Savonarola's death, the group known as Piagnoni originated in Florence to preserve its memory. Savonarola attracted the admiration of many later religious humanists, who valued his deep spiritual convictions.

Over the years, monuments to Savonarola were inaugurated in Ferrara, Bologna, and Florence.

He was not perfect, but he was undoubtedly looking for the good of all of Florence; he wanted all the citizens of Florence to go to heaven.

The history of Florence goes on. The Medicis return to power and continue to influence the city as they had done before.

From the descendants of the Medicis came Pope Leo X, whose secular name was Giovanni, son of Lorenzo and Clarice Medici. This pope decided to build St. Peter's Basilica. This construction demanded heavy investments in gold and silver, which were depleted in the coffers of the Church of Rome.

The church was heavily indebted at the time due to the excesses with which the church was run in that period. Since the coffers had to be filled anyway, the pope went to the sale of indulgences; under the promise of getting salvation in the afterlife. The pope published a bull asking for donations from the Christian faithful for the basilica work. The scandalous transaction of indulgences for money triggered Martin Luther to initiate 1517 an ecclesiastical reform that would split the Christian community.

The sale of indulgences forgave the penalty due for sins in exchange for a previously established payment.

Under this pope came Martin Luther with his writing of the 95 Theses. The condemnations of the Lutheran doctrines made by the pope and the ex-communication in 1521 of their author and those who followed them were useless: the Protestant Reformation could not be stopped.

Luther studied the Scriptures profoundly and immersed himself in studying the Bible and the early church. Luther was convinced that the church had lost sight of the various central truths that Christianity taught in the Scriptures, one of the most important of which was the doctrine of justification by faith alone. Luther began to teach that salvation is an exclusive gift given by grace through Christ and granted only by faith.

Luther defined and reintroduced the principle of the proper distinction between the Law of Moses and the Gospels, reinforcing the theology of grace.

"For it is by grace you have been saved, through faith- and this is not from yourselves, it is the gift of God- not by works, so that no one can boast" (Ephesians 2:8-9).

This truth began to spread throughout Europe. A Christian didn't have to buy anything; a Christian just had to believe and, by grace, receive. Repent from the heart and show such repentance by abandoning evil, a life of sin.

People began to read the Bible as it began to be propagated by the printing press. Everyone began to read the Bible in their language because it was then translated into German, English and other languages.

Time passed, and another Medici descendant emerged in the papacy under the name of Clement VII.

Curiously, Clement VII asked Michelangelo, the greatest painter of all time, to do one last work in the Sistine Chapel. Clement VII asked Michelangelo to paint "The Fall of the Rebels". The previous work that Michelangelo chose to make as a gift for the Medici would be "The Last Judgement".

It is as if Michelangelo consciously knew that we must all answer to God, and his last work wanted to leave us this message that it did not matter if you were a Medici, a Disalvatore, or a Habsburg. Someday, every one of us will answer to God. We shall all be answerable to God.

No matter your last name, no matter your race, no matter your social status, no matter your academic or cultural level, every one of us will be accountable to God. In that moment of total solemnity, it will matter to have the Advocate of lawyers on our side: Jesus, since only he can make us come out innocent from a case of which we are guilty, because we have all sinned, but only by grace can we be forgiven, cleansed and restored.

Allegria Disalvatore had made peace with God.

Giovanni Medici had made peace with God.

Costantino Habsburg died without making peace with God.

Allegria and Giovanni walked calmly daily because they knew their eternity was assured. They had believed in the one who could save them: Jesus. Heaven was waiting for them.

As Ephesians 3:12 says, "In him and through faith in him we may approach God with freedom and confidence". Allegria and

Giovanni were confident because, through faith, they had heaven on their side, heaven within their reach.

Allegria and Giovanni were happy every day of their lives, whatever their situation because they had learned to trust and walk with God at every moment. They were not perfect, but they were happy knowing they could pray, read the Bible and be guided by the excellent care of our God. The joy of the Lord was their strength.

It's incredible, but since God gives us as much good as the good that Allegria and Giovanni could enjoy every day, how is it that there are people who decide hell?

Jesus, in his immense love, took pity on Allegria's life and decided to take her out of the pit of despair to make her life a splendid reality, really live heaven on earth.

Since God can give you so much good, how come man chooses to get lost?

Costantino learned to believe what the system told him; he never understood the difference that you are not what you feel, that you are not what you do, that you must learn to believe what God says about you and not appropriate the title that the system gives you. For example, before Moses became the deliverer of a people, he was a murderer. However, Moses did not appropriate the identity of a murderer; he knew that God forgave him and developed his identity by the destiny that God gave him, that of being a liberator.

We are not what we do; we are what God says we are. We must learn to develop our identity based on how God sees us and how He defines us, not based on our sins.

God created each of us with a purpose that defines our identity. We are not our sins; we are based on the purpose for which God created us.

Sin is a destructive force that wants to divert us from the path of good, from the right way, so we must learn to fight against those forces that want to degrade us as people. Costantino never wanted to fight against these forces; he was always weak and surrendered to evil. Allegria always felt the same destructive forces, but she always knew how to shelter herself in Jesus so that He would give her the strength not to fall into evil. Two people, same situation, two different answers. Each of us chooses where we will spend eternity.

Costantino made the same mistake repeatedly; he fed on a destructive system that only strengthened more and these destructive forces; instead of running to God and the scriptures, he ran to everything that diverted him. There we can see the results.

If you know how to feed on the scriptures and the truth, those destructive forces will begin to lose power, control or influence, and you will have self-control and the strength to say "no" to evil. May it be in your life as it is in heaven, as Jesus prayed, "May it be on earth as it is in heaven".

Costantino did not know how to choose friends; he surrounded himself with evil, and sin consumed him. Because sound is contagious, just like evil, you must surround yourself with good people. Be wise and intelligent, surround yourself with pious people who fear God, who is kind and merciful, and your life will begin to emanate such goodness.

Each of us was born to reign, to exert a degree of positive influence on society. We may not be able to rule the world, but we can be a significant influence in our homes, families, places of study or work wherever God places you, wherever life takes you, you can be a testimony of God's truth.

As it is written, "Praise be to the Lord your God, who has delighted in you and placed you on the throne of Israel. Because of the Lord's eternal love for Israel, he has made you king to maintain justice and righteousness" (1 Kings 10:9). We may not be kings in Israel. Still, we can have a throne in that we all have an area to influence by doing good by practising what is right, whether in the family, place of study or work. We were all called to be kings or queens.

We are in the 21st century, but that does not mean that eternity has ceased to exist and that we are not on our way to destruction, that we do not have to review our position and repent of our courses that have been so twisted or deviated. It would do us no harm today to rekindle the "bonfire of vanities".

What should we burn on such a bonfire? Anything that doesn't fit these honourable descriptions.

It would be good to throw all our pride into the bonfire of vanities. "If anyone thinks they are something when they are not, they deceive themselves" (Galatians 6:3).

It would be good to throw into the bonfire of vanities all our lust or vanity that desires to make us the most beautiful or desirable, our excessive desire for power, all our ambition, all our arrogance and all our passion for earthly glories.

In the end, in this life, what matters is to respect God in everything and to obey his commands because that is the law of life: "to obey God in everything, to respect His person".

Allegria learned this lesson with pain, so she made these verses her life motto and meditated on these truths day and night.

All the days of her life, she repented of having been so foolish, so vain, having sought what she should not have sought, having caused her soul to descend into such deep sorrows in hell. Not a day went by that she didn't repent, ask God for forgiveness and thank God for this new opportunity.

"Those who work their land will have abundant food, but those who chase fantasies have no sense" (Proverbs 12:11). Allegria regretted having been a woman without so much understanding and was therefore determined to order her life and cultivate her land, to cultivate her life based on reason.

Allegria had cast into the bonfire of vanities all that had stopped her, all that had harmed her, all the evil she had done.

Allegria was determined to cleanse her life, and she did it, abandoning all vanity, all that was crooked and was deeply grateful to God for this new opportunity that God Himself had given her. Now she was so happy. She was pleased.

In this life, we must know how to eliminate from our lives everything that distances us from God. To carry all sin that separates us from authentic faith and heavenly life to the stake of vanities.

We must learn to eliminate everything that distances us from God. It would be good for us today to throw into that bonfire all that has so far stopped us from doing His will.

When Allegria burned all her sins, everything that stopped and paralyzed her to follow God, to follow the good and to walk in a life of holiness is when she could be happy and free.

When Allegria confessed her sins and turned away from evil, it was when she was truly free. Not only free from sin and evil but free from the power of all her enemies, she felt so pleased as she had never been in all her life.

Because sins become a lobby on a dead-end road, it's good to eliminate them.

At the end of his days, when death was upon him, Lorenzo, head of the most important family in Florence and all of Europe, thought only of this; he only wanted to be saved.

Because at the end of the day, in this life, when life is over, all that matters is making peace with God.

And you, do you have any sin to confess? Do you have any sins to throw into the bonfire of vanities?

And just like Pontius Pilate when he said "Ecce Homo," which would be "Here is the man", waiting for an answer from the others, today Jesus asks you the same question: "Here I'm, what will be your decision?"

Because before the Supreme Judge, we will no longer be able to confess, we will no longer be able to have "animus confident," which would be the power to make a statement, there before the Supreme Judge, we will only be able to hear our "acquittal" or our "condemnation". On this earth, one confesses and hears the final verdict in eternity.

Before God and before the law, when we are judged, we cannot say, "We did not know", for no matter how much we try to ignore God and His law, that day, He will judge us and determine whether we will spend eternity in heaven with Him or in hell with the fallen ones.

And you, where will you spend your eternity? Did you make peace with God? Do you have any sin to confess?